D0794051

The Lambs

THEIR LIVES, THEIR FRIENDS, AND THEIR CORRESPONDENCE

AMS PRESS
NEW YORK

The Lambs

THEIR LIVES, THEIR FRIENDS, AND THEIR CORRESPONDENCE

New Particulars and New Material

BY

WILLIAM CAREW HAZLITT

LONDON
ELKIN MATHEWS, VIGO STREET
NEW YORK
CHARLES SCRIBNER'S SONS
MDCCCXCVII

Library of Congress Cataloging in Publication Data

Hazlitt, William Carew, 1834-1913.
The Lambs.

1. Lamb, Charles, 1775-1834. 2. Lamb, Mary Ann, 1764-1847.
PR4863.H35 1973 824'.7 [B] 70-168955
ISBN 0-404-07369-7

Reprinted from the edition of 1897, New York
First AMS edition published, 1973
Manufactured in the United States of America

AMS PRESS, INC.
New York, N. Y. 10003

FAMILY AND FRIENDS

B

FAMILY AND FRIENDS

SEEING the eminence which Lamb had attained, and the arguable probability that the circumstances of his life and the biographical particulars relative to his parents and origin would become acceptable to future generations, it seems unaccountable, and indeed outrageous, that such men as Talfourd and Procter should have neglected, while it was possible to do so, to collect information and clues. Lamb himself voluntarily laid before the world a kind of *chiaroscuro* glimpse of the subject; with this in their hand, his friends might have readily taken him in communicative moods, and left us a body of facts, for which we should have been thankful indeed. No such matter. Nearly all that we know, we have to learn piecemeal, and much we shall never regain.

The fate of many other writers has overtaken Lamb, who, after experiencing in the earlier part of his career either obloquy or abuse, lived to see his most trivial productions almost fulsomely eulogised, while after his death many things, on which he and his friends could never have laid stress, were held up to admiration and applause. This passes for criticism; it is neither criticism nor justice, and it is extremely apt, besides, to misguide persons not intimate with the peculiar title of the Lambs to our deep and lasting regard.

Of the detached pieces of autobiography in the Essay form, the full worth has yet to be extracted and reduced to shape and method. Each successive labourer in the field culls something new, or strikes a fresh view. But they await a patient and exhaustive study. I am persuaded that within their limits many a doubt, many a moot point, many a missing link, may be solved or supplied by approaching them with a competent knowledge of the ground and the bearings.

It must be added that, in consulting the papers which thus shed light on Lamb's life and history, especial care should be taken to employ the true text, as liberties were occasionally taken even with the original impressions of *Elia* (1823-33), and what has been achieved since by

Bowdler, we can only surmise from his operations on the Letters.

It is scarcely the case, that the Essays could be woven into a complete and consecutive biographical sketch or view, as, after the most assiduous research, many gaps would remain; but they are susceptible of being profitably employed in filling up interstices, as it were, or as corroborative testimony.

An explanation and defence of my view may be found in the communication of Lamb, in 1826, to the *Every Day Book*, relevant to a previous paper on Captain Starkey. There the writer enters into graphic particulars of a little school in Fetter Lane, kept by Mr. William Bird, assisted by Captain Starkey, which Charles attended in the morning and his sister in the evening. I do not dwell farther on the account which he gives, and which Canon Ainger reproduces in his Biography. But I point to this as a sort of test case. How much was within the Lambs' recollection, which might have been similarly preserved, and which is at present irretrievably lost!

A knowledge of the father strikes me as imperative in judging how far the brother and sister influenced each other in the formation of a common literary taste, for Charles himself, her junior by so many years, was principally instrumental in stimulating his relative and life-companion. The ordinary conception of John Lamb the elder is that he was in a state of dotage; and there has never been much inclination to look below the surface. We have not far to go, nevertheless, to discover that the *prima stamina* of Lamb's faculty and his sister's were resident in their male parent, and that the feeling for art and letters was shared by the elder brother. It was a delicate and fragile germ, which, under unfavourable conditions, might have withered and perished, but which in two cases out of three—in one very conspicuously—developed and fructified. In cases where the literary faculty or any species of intellectual development has manifested itself in an individual, it is usual to assume and to seek the source of the gift or the power; nor is the absence of a germ to be inferred because the clue to it is not forthcoming. With many great English characters there are no known data for forming an opinion. The father of the three Lambs, Mr. John Lamb, Scrivener, though a man of humble education and imperfect training, clearly possessed some tincture of literary feeling; and he possessed a few books—the slenderest and poorest nucleus of a library. If researches could be undertaken among the parish registers of Lincolnshire and Hertfordshire, it might transpire that the family once enjoyed a better status: the episode of the rich relative, to whom Aunt Hetty was sent for a while in 1796, furnishes a hint of some such thing.

Poetry of a moral or religious cast appears to have been the bent of the father.* Southey had under his eyes the volume written by him; but it has not been recovered. From Southey's slight account we collect that it was the prototype of the *Poetry for Children*. It would be interesting to stumble upon a copy; for it must exist, if it was printed. Its sole conceivable worth would be genealogical, as it were.

From the mention of John Lamb the father as a scrivener, it might have been supposed that he belonged to the Gild of that name; but a search undertaken for the purpose by Mr. Wootton for me quite recently resulted in a failure to discover any person of the name within the period. Mr. Lamb was therefore probably only a copyist or clerk, and not technically a scrivener at all.

* Hazlitt's Edition of the Letters, 1886, I., 3–4.

Of the circumstances under which John Lamb and, during a short time, his younger brother obtained a footing in the South Sea House, we know nothing; but it may be mentioned that Mr. Thomas Coventry, one of the Members of the Inner Temple, and a colleague in that sense of Samuel Salt, the elder Lamb's employer, was a large holder of South Sea Stock, of which he presented £10,000 in 1782 to Christ's Hospital, and it may have been through his agency that the two Lambs were engaged.

John Lamb, the *James Elia* of literary history, presents himself to our scrutiny as little more than a dim figure in the background. We learn next to nothing of his individuality; and the few landmarks in his obscure career are derived altogether from scattered notices in the Essays and Letters, except that to Hazlitt and Talfourd we owe some account of his attendance at the Wednesdays in the Temple and his argumentative propensity. He occupied chambers during several years in the upper part of the South Sea House subsequently to its disestablishment and conversion into chambers and offices, and his retirement on a pension. He shared his father's and brother's literary taste, and wrote a treatise on *Humanity to Animals*; and he was more or less of a connoisseur in paintings. The portrait of Milton, which he bought in 1815, and bequeathed to Charles, is now in the National Portrait Gallery; he was rather addicted to this class of collecting, but his other works of art went for a song.

John Lamb ultimately married a widow with some property and a daughter, and the wife of a Mr. Isaac Dowden; but he predeceased her, dying in November, 1821, and unconsciously bequeathing to his brother a suit at law in connection with the Dowden estate. He is described in the Elian paper on *Dream-Children*, in the *London Magazine* for January, 1822, as no more. His death is mentioned in Lamb's letter to Wordsworth of March 20, 1822.

The South Sea House, desolate and silent as it was in Lamb's day, when he penned the famous essay upon it, is tenfold more degraded at present. It has been partly dismantled, and partly transformed, till scarcely any vestige of the original building, as the two Lambs knew it, remains. The board-room has been partitioned off into clerks' offices. Some of the books are in the cellars under Threadneedle Street; some are in the British Museum.

The portrait of Milton reminds me of that of Shakespear, described in the letter to Barron Field of September 22, 1822. It was the spurious likeness of the poet palmed off upon Talma the actor for £40, or 1000 francs, and the authenticity of which Lamb, I apprehend, did not altogether disbelieve.

It was surely the same piece of imposture to which we find a clue in some Ireland MSS. which were sold by public auction on the 11th February, 1886, and from which we collect that the pair of bellows, with its *vera effigies*, was in 1820 in the possession of a gentleman, who had received from Mr. Ireland junior an offer of £80 for them. The owner, whose name has been cut off from his letter in reply, dates from Wood's Hotel, Arundel Street, Haymarket, June 28, 1820. The inscription accompanying the picture varied from that given by Lamb to Field. No doubt the forgery was identical with that mentioned, and Talma was considered a likely and easy dupe, as indeed he proved. Perhaps the most singular part of the affair is or was, that Lamb, for the only time in his life, should have been on the spot just at the particular juncture, and it is some tribute to the ingenuity of the fabricator, that a man, who might have been taken to be something of a judge, was dubious on the point.

The personal history of Lamb's brother is still more obscure than that of John Lamb the elder. Both are to be gleaned to a large extent, so far as we can ever know them, from casual and almost inadvertent references in the Elian writings. The brother's book on *Humanity to Animals*, of which Charles is found sending a copy to Crabb Robinson in or about 1810, with a view to obtaining a notice in the press, has not been identified, although it must have been published, and Lamb even gives the publisher's name—Wilson. Curiously enough, in a series of tracts called the *Cottage Library of Christian Knowledge*, is one entitled, "Humanity to Animals Recommended." It consists of twelve pages only, and is chiefly made up of quotations from Cowper and others. The topic was one which was beginning to engage attention. The *brochure* just cited is not that of which we are in quest.

John Lamb cannot have been an old man when he died; he is stated, in the letter to Robinson, to be "a plump, good-looking man of seven-and-forty."

The trace to the elder Lamb of some faint intellectual inspiration does not greatly assist us, however, in solving the origin of his illustrious son's extraordinary attainments as a letter-writer, as a critic, and as a wit. For that part of the unique story we have, I apprehend, to go to his early associations and to the force of fellowship and generous rivalry operating on a powerful and receptive understanding. It is not very difficult, when we reflect a little, to see how the mental training through which Lamb passed by his successive intercourse with James White, the two Le Grices, Coleridge, Lloyd, Southey, and Manning, both personally and on paper, was apt to yield fruit, and to develope the actual results. He met his friends at intervals face to face; but it was a curious coincidence that most of them resided at a distance from London, and that the consequent difficulty of communication necessitated a resort to the post, and with it the growth of a habit of committing thoughts to writing, until it may be questionable whether Lamb did not acquire greater facility for expressing himself in that way than by word of mouth.

Quite enough has been made and heard of

Lamb as a miscellaneous writer, and I deprecate the tendency to regard him as a mere humourist. But his correspondence must remain an integral part of the age, which it immediately concerns, as much as that of Walpole; and in this capacity and aspect, if in no other, he has laid himself, so to speak, across an epoch. Any one who bestows even a cursory study on these inimitable productions must perceive and allow that the serious style largely preponderates, and that of broad fun there is little more than an occasional vein. His wit is more usually delicate and playful—sometimes bordering on pathos. Here and there, among the letters, there are spasms of boisterous and rollicking gaiety parallel with the horse-play in the Inner Temple Lane times; but it makes little indeed in so voluminous a body of matter.

It has often struck me that, if the veil could be lifted by some enchantment from the obscurity which hangs over the humble lodgings of Lamb and his parents in Little Queen Street, of the structural character of which we are only enabled to judge from the few buildings, adjoining the site, which still survive, a good deal of light might be cast on the foundations of the Lamb correspondence. We do not merely suffer from the absence—with exceptions hardly worth mentioning—of the entire *corpus* of letters directed to Lamb from the very outset, but the eighteenth century domestic annals, leaving out of account the sad tragedy of 1795, are almost a blank. Their history is made up of glimpses from Lamb's letters to Coleridge, and the gleanings of Talfourd, who, had he even known the family earlier, was neither very curious nor very careful. I may render my meaning clearer by saying that, if Lamb had had a Cottle or an Alsop, we should have been apprised of a variety of facts, and have been in possession of documents rendering the narrative of these dark days infinitely more luminous and connected.

In the first place, I am somewhat sceptical as to the commonly-received account of John Lamb the father—the Lovel of the *Essays*. In fact, the Essayist's account of his father, as he was in earlier life, is precisely what does not seem to tally with the notion of his lowness of origin; and his wife was at least respectably allied, to whatever the description of Lamb may amount, where he employs the term "rich" as characteristic of the Fields. They were, no doubt, so by comparison.

John Lamb evidently possessed a taste for books and letters. His copies of *Hudibras*, 1726, and of a volume of the *Guardian*, 1750, were preserved by his son. The latter had his autograph mark of ownership in 1756, when he must have been about thirty years of age. The portrait of him, engraved in the Biography by Procter, 1866, conveys the idea of a man of forty or so; it is not unlike the style of Hancock, but it was too early for that artist. It was surely taken when he was in his prime, as he is sketched in *Elia*, and when he committed to the press his *Poetical Pieces on Several Occasions*, the volume seen by Southey when he visited Little Queen Street in 1795.

Nevertheless, here is a personage who is presented to our view, under the shadow of *Lovel*, as a humourist, an angler, a cribbage-player, a self-taught mechanic, and a fine manly spirit; whom we see to have been the producer of a volume of verses, of which the sample published by Talfourd is perfectly in unison with the metrical effusions of his son, and of whom there is a portrait extant; and, although such a knowledge would have been eminently valuable, we have to satisfy readers and the public with inferential conjectures drawn from incidental or obscure allusions. Had it not been for the autobiographical group of papers in *Elia* and elsewhere, for a few waifs and strays in Talfourd, and the early correspondence, it is not too much to affirm that we should have remained almost completely ignorant of the parentage and descent of Lamb; and those papers, it should be recollected, were not compiled for the purpose of conveying personal information, which they, in fact, do their best to disguise, but of yielding topics for periodicals.

Lamb left Christ's Hospital, as we all know pretty well by this time, in 1789, but the exact circumstances of his first entrance there and his departure from it are not so generally familiar. Indeed, we have never yet seen any account of these incidents. From the admission-books of the Hospital, it appears that Charles Lamb, son of John Lamb, scrivener, was admitted by a bond for £100, under the hand of Samuel Salt, Esq., on the presentation of Timothy Yeats, Esq., in 1782. He was admitted July 17, but not *clothed* till October 9, the Temple being extra-parochial, and security being therefore demanded for the boy's due discharge. But the most remarkable point is the form in which that discharge is made out:—

"1789, Novr. 23. Charles Lamb is this day discharged from this Hospital for ever by Elizabeth Lamb his Mother living in the Temple, who is to provide a Master for him."

[Signed] Eliz. Lamb.

Why the father did not come forward has still to be ascertained. The document which I now first make public is incontestably curious and interesting. Was the father already in failing health? In 1782, in the form of presentation, he, as the petitioner, had described himself as a person with a wife and three children, with inadequate resources for their education.

Not more than half a dozen years, we thus see, intervened between the removal of the boy by his mother and the mournful event which led him to undertake the charge of his sister during the remainder of his life.

Looking at the signature of Mrs. Lamb to the entry in the admission-books, one is struck by the similarity of the character to the writing of her son. Talfourd tells us that he acquired his clerkly style of caligraphy at the India House. Of course the *Eliz. Lamb* of the official memorandum is merely a signature.

In the very threshold of the Stoddart series of letters, in one of September 3, 1803, we see that there was a disparity of social standing between John Lamb and his wife, and another hint is given of the same thing in the essay on "Poor Relations." The bookbinder was a kinsman on the paternal side; but we own such fragmentary and disjointed *data* for handling this part of the subject, that it is futile—at any rate here—to pursue the inquiry.

The two-fold agency of the literary article, based on the personal history of the author, and of the letters of the first period (1796—1800), commending themselves to the recipients as storehouses of criticism on their own work, has mainly saved the opening of Lamb's career from being involved in utter darkness. The particulars, which we find ourselves enabled to gather from Talfourd, and one or two other sources, are marvellously scanty.

Yet in these days, now so far in retrospect, when the family lived at 7, Little Queen Street (1782—99), it was no insignificant circle which had formed itself round them, humble and poor as they were. Let us think what visitors they are likely, or more than so, to have had. There was James White, the two Le Grices, Coleridge, the Lloyds, Norris (the father's friend before he was the son's), and Dyer. Between these (and others, of whom the record is deficient) and the Lambs there must have been occasional intercourse and friendly sociable greeting. A considerable number of letters must have been exchanged in the space of so many years. Without reckoning trivial notes, that interval witnessed the beginning of the correspondence with Coleridge, Southey, Lloyd, and Manning. It has all apparently perished.

Nor have we a vestige of anything in written likeness directed to the two Le Grices, to White, or to that elder brother, who soon took the resolution of quitting the paternal roof, and eventually found quarters in the South Sea House Chambers. That we do not possess many letters to Norris and Dyer is, so far, less surprising, since they were both within call, and yet, again, we have had handed down to us (preserved by the merest accident) one or two epistles to the latter as long and as journal-like as though they had been intended for Manning at Canton.

On a deliberate consideration of all the circumstances, it seems simply incredible that we may not hope, from time to time, to receive salvage, at least, from the wreck of valuable literary and biographical material formed between 1789 and the close of the century. The letters which have periodically occurred at public sales in the course of the last twenty or thirty years, one by one, render me individually rather sanguine of greater discoveries; for, as a rule, the additional items are so far either the originals of printed letters, or are autographs belonging to a later epoch, such as those first published by Canon Ainger to Chambers, Dodwell, Dibdin, and Mrs. Kenney. It is delightful to have regained them, but they are not quite what we mean and what we want.

The Lloyd papers are now ascertained to be at all events partially extant, and may be expected to appear in type; I shall return to this point presently. We seem to hold as much as we can expect to see of the Manning, except in the way of collation. Whether any Coleridge MSS. of this class, anterior to May, 1796, exist, is somewhat uncertain. The survival of Le Grice letters is possible. Of earlier ones to Dyer, and of any to John Lamb, we may almost despair.

The wealthy and significant nature of the epistolary intercourse between Miss Lamb and Miss Stoddart will fortify my statement—as it does my belief—that if even a proportion of the stores just indicated could be recovered, they would exhibit an interest and value immeasurably above any new matter in Ainger or Hazlitt. We may be pleased enough to get letters to more recent correspondents; but as the spring is to the river, such to the maturer history of the Lambs would be the ampler record of their existence, wretched and indigent as it may have been, in Little Queen Street, to the more comfortable and more familiar life in the Temple, in Covent Garden, at Islington, and at Enfield.

Infinitely more singular, however, than the mystery enveloping the period to which I refer, is that which we experience, years afterward, respecting the movements of the brother and sister. Not all the correspondence, not all the collateral sources of knowledge, tend to explain very clearly what the Lambs were doing in 1804, in 1807, and between 1811 and 1813. Those years bear the same relation to their biography that 1745—6 do to that of Johnson. In their case letters are of the fewest and references of the most meagre. All of which we can be positively sure is that they were unusually full of literary work, and they presumably held their Wednesdays. I touch on this curious point elsewhere.

Of the visiting circle at Little Queen Street about 1796, Coleridge, the two Le Grices, Dyer, and White were brother Crugs. Leigh Hunt was also of Christ's Hospital, but Lamb and he did not meet again till a much later date, when Hunt was in prison for an alleged libel on the Prince Regent from February, 1813, to February, 1815, and the Lambs went to visit him, as he says in his *Autobiography*, in all weathers, even in the severe winter of 1813-14. In 1816, Hunt included Lamb among the recipients of the *Story of Rimini*, and the letter, acknowledging the receipt of the volume, is or was preserved. But the acquaintance never became very intimate, though Hunt is described by Hazlitt as amongst the Wednesday men.

On the contrary, the friendship with White and the Le Grices appears, so far as I can make out, to have been almost exclusively confined to Little Queen Street days; and Lamb's feeling toward White, as he confesses in a letter to Coleridge of 1798, was never one of unqualified trust and cordiality. He chiefly admired his intellectual turn.

George Dyer,* who survived till 1841, was the

*For these and other similar unpublished particulars I was indebted, many years since, to the courtesy of Mr. A. W. Lockhart, Steward of Christ's Hospital.

son of John Dyer, citizen and shipwright of London, and was born on the 15th March, 1755. He was admitted July 1st, 1762, from the Precinct of Bridewell, was sent to Emmanuel College, Cambridge, in 1774, and took his B.A. degree in 1778.

Charles Valentine Le Grice, and his brother Samuel, sons of Frederick Franklin Le Grice, of Trereife, Cornwall, were respectively admitted in 1792 and 1794. The former went into the Church; the latter served in the Peninsula during the War, and succumbed to the climate. Valentine Le Grice printed at Penzance privately in 1803 a version of the *Daphnis and Chloe* of Longus. He remained at Trereife through the remainder of a very long life, during the latter part of which he was in the enjoyment of affluence through his marriage with a lady of fortune. In the subjoined letter to Lord Lyndhurst, written in March, 1858, he gives an interesting account of himself and his family:—

"A mile from Penzance to the West,
Trereife (pronounced Treve).

"My Dear Lord Lyndhurst,—Your letter with satisfactory corrections of my error with respect to your health has excited in me the most lively pleasure. You kindly inquire for some account of myself. My history is happily uniform. I am where I came in 1796, and am now, by marriage in 1799 with the mother of my pupil, possessor of an ample estate, my pupil having bequeathed it to his mother. He lived to the twenty-eighth year of his age, only partially relieved from his weakness, but free from pain. I have been a widower for thirty years. I have a son in fine health nearly sixty years of age, and a grandson who is now at Oriel College, where his father was before him. The volume of which I beg your acceptance will convey a history of my movements. I was minister of Penzance—a perpetual curacy, small emolument—for twenty-eight years.* I have no duty now, nor would undertake any. I am now, and ever have been, in excellent health. I never walk to fatigue myself, but am *agilis*. I have reason to be, as I am, most grateful. I am a magistrate, and so is my son. I do not sleep so well as I was wont to do. My estate on which I reside is in view of the sea, without interruption, nor possibility of it. I think I told you that Agnipedes [Archdeacon Sheepshanks] for the latter years of his life was within twenty miles of me. I used to come in contact with dear Jones [see Wordsworth's sonnet, which begins: "Jones, as from Calais southward you and I"]. My sermons by locality, &c., will fill up my history.—Dear Lord Lyndhurst, Accept my dearest regards. Yours sincerely, C. Val de Grice."

James White, the hero of the *Falstaff Letters*, was the son of Samuel White, of Bewdley,

*The Le Grice family was still located at Trereife in 1872.

Worcestershire, and was baptized April 17th, 1775, having been born, it thus seems, in the same year as Lamb himself. He was admitted to Christ's Hospital on the presentation of Thomas Coventry, Esquire, September 19th, 1783, and was discharged on the 30th April, 1790, in order to be taken into the Treasurer's office, where he remained some years. He subsequently founded or joined an advertizing agency in Fleet Street, which still survives under the old name.

The James White, *Esquire*, who published, between 1789 and 1791, three or four books of a semi-historical character, and who made a tour in Wales in 1740, I take to have been related to Samuel White, and to be the James White who, in 1759, brought out a version of the *Clouds* of Aristophanes, dating his epistle before the work from Cecil Street, Strand. A copy of this scarce volume was in Lamb's collection, not very rich in classical authors; and in the preface to another of his publications he indulges in a quaint, pleasant vein, reminding us of the perpetrator of the Falstaff hoax.

I am treading on rather new ground, and must not hazard too much in the way of conjecture. But James White the elder, if we may so term him, was apparently a teacher, and produced a grammatical treatise in 1761, shortly after his Aristophanes. It is scarcely probable that he had any concern with the firm in Fleet Street. The British Museum Catalogue describes his presumed nephew as "a *newspaper* agent."

Charles Lloyd was the son of a cadet of a Montgomeryshire family of the same name. This younger branch joined the Society of Friends, and settled tolerably early in the last century at Birmingham as iron-masters and bankers. Charles Lloyd did not care to go into the business, and his younger brother James took his place, Charles receiving an allowance from the father. He married early—when he was about 23—Sophia Pemberton, who was still younger, about 20, and they lived at first in the Lake Country, where their eldest son was born in 1800, but subsequently at Moseley, near Birmingham, where Lamb visited them more than once. The Olivia of the *Letters* was Lloyd's sister; she married P. M. James, the banker. I owe to the kindness of Dr. Garnett the curious fact that Lloyd found a valuable distraction from his mental troubles in a performance by Macready of an impersonation of a similar malady, and wrote a copy of verses (still in MS.) commemorative of his relief and his gratitude.

The Lloyd papers, which at one time were said to have perished, have been quite recently discovered in two parts, one at Birmingham, the other at Nottingham; they extend to some hundreds of documents: but the interest centres in about seventeen letters from Lamb to Lloyd himself, the rest being letters from Manning, and from numbers of the Lloyd family, and chiefly important from their incidental mention of Lamb.

Charles Lloyd the younger, born in 1800, and a son of the poet, died in 1873, and was buried at Chiswick.

A fairly complete list of Lloyd's works is given by me in the *Mary and Charles Lamb* volume, 1874, But it omits the folio volume of Poems on the death of his grandmother, Priscilla Farmer, 1796, of which one value is to shew that at that time Lamb and Lloyd had not yet met; and A Letter to the Anti-Jacobin Reviewers, 4to, Birmingham, 1799, in the appendix to which occurs a most interesting reference to Lamb:—

"The person you have thus leagued in a partnership of infamy with me is Mr. Charles

Lamb, a man who, so far from being a democrat, would be the first person to assent to the opinions contained in the foregoing pages: he is a man too much occupied with real and painful duties—duties of high personal self denial—to trouble himself about speculative matters.

"Whenever he has thrown his ideas together, it has been from the irresistible impulse of the moment, never from any intention to propagate a system, much less any 'of folly and wickedness.'"

This is in the right vein, and does as much honour to the writer as it does justice to the subject of the remarks.

The readers of the Lamb letters can hardly fail to have become familiar with the name of Norris. Lamb knew him as he knew none besides. He was his and his father's friend for nearly half a century, he tells Southey in 1823. When John Lamb became so that he was scarcely any longer a companion, Norris was next—in a sense, he was nearer. When the mother fell by the daughter's hand, Charles wrote to Coleridge (September 27, 1796): "Mr. Norris, of the Bluecoat School, has been very kind to us, and *we have no other friend*."

In his next communication to the same, a few days later, he says: "Mr. Norris, of Christ's Hospital, has been as a father to me, Mrs.

Norris as a mother, though we had few claims on them."

In the Christmas of 1825 Norris lay on his dying bed. Ever since his boyhood Lamb had spent that day with him and Mrs. Norris. He came from witnessing the closing scene in the saddest of moods, and the trouble and sense of bereavement were such as he had never before experienced. He writes to Crabb Robinson, January 20, 1826: "In him I have a loss the world cannot make up. He was my friend and my father's friend all the life I can remember. I seem to have made foolish friendships ever since. Those are friendships which outlast a second generation. Old as I am waxing, in his eyes I was still the child he first knew me. To the last he called me Charley. I have none to call me Charley now. He was the last link that bound me to the Temple. You are but of yesterday."

Norris had very special claims on Lamb's tender and enduring regard. Even when he was a little shy, delicate school-boy, the under-treasurer at the Inner Temple, his father's friend, used to procure him *exeats* extraordinary from the Christ's Hospital precinct, and enable him to enjoy many a half-holiday either in

Crown Office Row or under his own roof; and Lamb furnishes more than a hint that this favouritism was rather apt to kindle in the bosoms of those who had no such good fairy at hand a passing sentiment of jealousy, more particularly as poor Aunt Hetty used also to bring to the cloisters just about the dinner-hour, when there was something more than usually savoury at her brother's frugal table, a plate of viands wrapped up in a kerchief, and sit down in a corner, kind soul, while the child ate his home-perfumed meal.

It seemed almost requisite to state so much, since there may be some who would not at once appreciate the peculiar importance of the little batch of letters, which I furnish below, in the presence of such an imposing array of correspondence with some of the most eminent characters of the age. But these stand *per se*, as Mr. and Mrs. Norris did.

I understand that the Inn, probably through the friendly offices of Crabb Robinson, settled on Mrs. Norris an annuity of £80.

There is a further consideration to be offered in this case. The letters of Mary Lamb belong to the period of her chequered and prolonged life, when her correspondence is of the rarest occurrence, and from the last item in the series it will be apparent that they were among her latest efforts to put her thoughts on paper. She did not long survive the note which Miss James addressed on her behalf to Miss Norris.

I may be right in ascribing the postponement of any knowledge, down to a quite recent date, that letters passed between the Lambs and the oldest of their friends, to the presumed absence of any sympathy with literary matters on the part of Norris and his family; and the surprising part, perhaps, is that they should have been preserved even in rather indifferent condition.

We have not to deal with Thomas Manning in any light except in that in which Lamb has made us see him. As the matter stands, he is one of the pillars of the correspondence; and the question arises when it commenced, and through whom the two were made acquainted in the first instance. Canon Ainger states that Lloyd introduced Manning to Lamb in the autumn of 1799; I say that it was when he visited Lloyd at Cambridge in the winter of that year that he met Manning. Now, the Canon appears to err in placing the letter dated December 28, 1799, before the undated one, which comes next in his book; for the undated one is almost assuredly the prior. In the former, Lamb mentions that he had "suspended his correspondence a decent interval," while in the other he emphatically says, "I must not prove tedious to you *in my first outset.*" In the Hazlitt arrangement, therefore, the letter of December 28 takes the second place.

Canon Ainger is to be congratulated, upon the whole, on the additional light which he has thrown on the personal history of Manning, and on the improved form in which he has been enabled by the family to give that very prominent feature in the earlier portion of the Lamb correspondence. Yet it is to be more than feared that the new matter has not been rendered fully and faithfully.

From a letter to Manning of December 5, 1806, we safely augur that Tuthill was an early friend of the Holcrofts, and had perhaps been of substantial service to the dramatist and his wife in their checkered career. Tuthill furnished Lamb with his certificate in 1825, but we hear of him only in a casual or incidental way. At his house Manning stayed at a later period, and it was to that address Moxon was instructed to send a copy of the second series of *Elia*, 1833, to "the

Chinese philosopher," then returned for good from his travels, uneaten by the "Man-Chew" Tartars.

Coleridge was the original medium of contact with the Cottles and Gutch at Bristol, and with Holcroft and Godwin in London; and Holcroft and Godwin, again, were instrumental in bringing him forward and establishing him as a member of that Jacobinical coterie which included in its ranks or on its skirts Stoddart, the two Hazlitts, Crabb-Robinson, Thelwall, Scarlett, and perhaps Mackintosh. Through Robinson he knew the Williams family at Farnham; through Holcroft or his wife the Kenneys, and through them, again, Howard Payne.

There were some with whom his early efforts in journalism made him temporarily acquainted —Fell and Fenwick, and others, such as Miss Mary Hays, the Godwins' friend.

I believe that I am right in saying that it was through Godwin that Lamb became acquainted with Stoddart and Hazlitt the miniature-painter, and that Lamb and Godwin were brought together by Coleridge. We observe in the letter of February 19th, 1803, to Manning, that it was at Rickman's that Lamb apparently first fell in with Burney. Lamb names the Wednesday

Evenings as a new institution, in a letter to Manning, of December 5, 1806. They were, at a later time, changed to Thursday. The *Thursdays* are specifically named in a letter of 1826 to Hazlitt, first printed in a very recent edition of the Correspondence. But the change from Wednesday had been made since 1817.

To George Dyer Lamb owed some obligations of this character, notably the friendship of John Rickman—an acquisition, which he notifies to Manning with evident satisfaction in 1800; and Rickman introduced the Burneys—James Burney, son of Dr. Burney, of musical fame, and brother of Fanny Burney, afterwards Madame D'Arblay, and Martin Burney, the Admiral's son, for whom Lamb entertained a rather whimsical regard. At a later date, in 1815, it was that his official colleague, Mr. William Evans, brought Lamb and Talfourd together. A few, like Bernard Barton, took the initiative themselves on some literary plea.

Admiral Burney, one of the most notable of the circle which collected round the Lambs, in Temple Lane, lived in James Street, Buckingham Gate, and the Lamb set used sometimes to meet there. His son Martin, who had some engagement on the press, lodged at one time in Fetter

Lane. He, too, had occasional evenings at home, and my father recollects well the cold boiled beef and porter for supper. Of the latter, Colonel Phillips, another of the whist-boys, was a copious partaker. Martin's housekeeper was a Mrs. McInnis, a tall, raw-boned Irishwoman: my father told me she was a fair cook, and had an odd way of saying "os becount of," instead of *because*.

Evans was a very old acquaintance. He entered the India House in 1796. He was related to the family, whose friendship with Coleridge is supposed to have led to the abrupt departure of the latter from Jesus College, in 1794. The object of the poet's attachment was Mary Evans, who is believed to have been one of the daughters of Thomas Evans, citizen and patten-maker, of London, whose brother Henry carried on business in King Street, Cheapside. They were of Montgomeryshire descent, and a John Evans was admitted to Christ's Hospital from that part.

A few letters to John Rickman are given in the editions; but others remain unprinted. One is in reference to an article by Lamb, in the *Morning Post*, on Shakespear's *Richard III*. The late Mr. Dykes Campbell had the use of them, with the proviso that they were not to be printed.

John and Thomas Clio Rickman appear, like so many other early acquaintances, to have owed their knowledge of the Lambs to John Hazlitt, who painted a portrait of the latter, a bookseller, stationer, and printer in Upper Marylebone Street, before 1800, in the February of which year it was engraved by James Holmes. My great-uncle also executed a miniature of the same person, which is among those in my possession.

Lamb was clearly pretty intimate with John Rickman in 1802, and perchance they became known to each other through Norris. Rickman and Burney were of the original Wednesday set. There is an inedited note from Lamb to the former, in which he addresses him as *Dear R.*, and in which he asks him to meet him at Norris's, saying: "I owe you 3*s.* 6*d.*, which I want to take out of you at Picquet."

One of the most noteworthy accessions to the stock was the recovery of two letters from Lamb himself to Charles and John Chambers respectively in 1817—18; and this find led to the further revelation on inquiry that they belonged to a series, of which others exist, and who the recipients were. One of these letters—that to Charles Chambers—has been published by the writer; the other Canon Ainger inserts (with omissions) in his edition of the Letters.

Thomas, Charles, Edward, John, and Mary Chambers were the children of the Rev. Thomas Chambers, Vicar of Radway-Edgehill, Warwickshire, a friendly and hospitable man, who loved good cheer, and who left a diary, in which he has recorded little beyond the dinners he used to give or eat. He speaks in one place of having been cured of a fit of the gout by a splendid lobster and some fine port given him by Lord Willoughby. All his family died unmarried. John and Charles Chambers were at Christ's Hospital; the former was subsequently a colleague of Lamb at the India House, and Charles, probably by the influence of his uncle, Admiral Chambers, became a surgeon in the Royal Navy, eventually retiring to Leamington, where he practised till his death, about 1857, as a medical man. John built the school at Radway, and Charles the Working Men's Club. The career of Edward was fixed by a curious incident which happened to Mr. James Broadwood, of the firm in Great Pulteney Street, during a stay in Warwickshire for coursing or hunting purposes. He lost his way toward nightfall one day, and asked a gentleman whom he met the road to the nearest inn. The gentleman was the Vicar of Radway, and he took him to his own house for the night. The result was that Edward Chambers became after a while cashier at Broadwood's, and remained so till his death. He was of the Mercers' Company, and gave some offence to the worshipful court by instituting financial inquiries. It is Admiral Chambers, who (with other members of the circle) is commemorated by John Moultrie in his "Dream of Life;" and the Vicar was "the sensible clergyman in Warwickshire," of whom we hear in the Elian essay, "Thoughts on Presents of Game." The Rev. Thomas Chambers married a Miss Miller, related to the Major Miller who, when his colonel was disabled, commanded the Enniskillen Dragoons at Waterloo.

John Chambers was the last survivor of all these; he died at his house at Lee, in Kent, in 1872. He kept a hospitable table, and was a liberal and intelligent man. He once subscribed £500 to a church rebuilding fund; but he used to say that if he knew a man who went to church three times a day, he would lock up the spoons from him. He rode up to the India House on a white horse during several years, and was so punctual that people regulated their watches by his movements. An old Warwickshire custom, which he observed, was to leave the dinner-table with his friends with full bottles, instead of making a point of clearing everything off. He had a peculiar fashion, when he rode in a carriage, of placing his servant inside, and riding on the box, because, as he said, his object was to get the fresh air. He is the *Ch.* of the "Superannuated Man."

John Chambers, the colleague of Lamb, used to relate many stories of his distinguished friend; three or four were lately printed in *Macmillan's Magazine;* and he would mention some singular facts about the doings in Leadenhall Street in the old days. One of the clerks occasionally kept a couple of hounds under his desk. Another who, like Chambers, rode on horseback to the office, missed his animal one day, and Lamb threw out a sly hint that Chambers knew something about the affair, so that the latter was watched, wherever he went, by two Bow Street runners, till the owner was told that his property had been seen in a stable in the north of London; and there he duly found it, and had to pay a fortnight's bait.

One remark of Lamb, handed down by his contemporary, was that he thought he must be the only man in England who had never worn boots and never mounted a horse.

Whatever may be the worth of these memorabilia, we have have set them down, because till quite recently even the name of Chambers was unknown to the biographers and readers of Lamb, and they possess a certain interest in themselves. They were most obligingly communicated to the present writer by Mr. Algernon Black, who was executor both to Charles and John. Mr. Black is of opinion that much of the pose of Lamb as a *bon viveur* was pure humour, and that as a matter of fact he was a moderate eater and drinker, and very little in the way of liquor affected him. More than twenty years ago I expressed a similar view.

Of Edward White, of the India House, to whom there is a letter in Hazlitt's edition, some account may be found in Cope's Reminiscences, 1891.* White lived at one time at Chelsea, near the bridge, where Cope visited him; but he probably died at Twickenham.

Cope's account of White, and what he says of Lamb, is worth reading. White was long one of the Wednesday set.

* Reminiscences of Charles West Cope, R.A. 8vo., 1891, p. 36—8.

Lamb appears to have known, presumably through Janus Weathercock, otherwise Griffiths Wainewright, the Abercromby family, with which Wainewright was connected by marriage. He thought highly of Wainewright as a writer, by virtue, perhaps, of the power of contrast, and letters may have passed between the two. They have not been found. But Lamb wrote verses in Madeleine Abercromby's album, and this production we have also, it seems, yet to rescue. We appear to be unable to do more than snatch back one by one strayed Letters and other remains.

Of the numerous correspondents of the Lambs it becomes the less surprising that we know in many cases comparatively little, when we reflect that, with certain illustrious and eminent exceptions, they were persons of no general celebrity. But it is vexatious to be so powerless in elucidating some of the sources of acquaintance, and the mode and order in which such distinguished men as Charles Lloyd, Manning, aud one or two more, gained a personal knowledge of Lamb and his sister, and entered into epistolary relations with him or them both. Of course Lamb's schoolfellow, Coleridge, was, as it were, the *primum mobile* in introducing him to Wordsworth, Southey, and Lloyd, and it appears to have been through the last-named that he first knew Manning. Southey was at Little Queen Street as early as 1795, in Mrs. Lamb's lifetime.

The Eastern Counties were remarkably fertile in yielding friends and correspondents. Manning himself was a younger son of the Rector of Diss, in Norfolk, and was Lamb's senior by three years. Crabb Robinson came from Bury St. Edmunds. Fornham gave Mrs. Williams. Then there was Barton at Woodbridge.

The series of letters between 1822 and 1830 to the Quaker clerk-poet at Woodbridge, Bernard Barton, are especially prizeable, because they present the writer in a level serious mood, and we see him on his *best behaviour*. The most fastidious editors have found nothing there of an exceptionable tenor. In his correspondence with others, with whom he was equally intimate, he is humorous, broad, even latitudinarian; but here he treads upon eggs; and yet how much poorer we should be without this matter! Some of Lamb's prettiest and daintiest, and tenderest thoughts, and some of his finest critical touches, lie among those epistles to Barton, and precious as they are to us, how unspeakably so must they have been to him!

In the letter to Barton of May 15, 1824, on the works of William Blake, I committed one serious error, when, in my edition of the Correspondence, 1886, I printed *Welch* for *Water* Paintings, having transcribed the production under difficult circumstances; but otherwise the text was taken for the first time from the autograph, the original having long left the hands of the Barton family.

Occasional allusions are found throughout the correspondence to Dyer, Norris, the Le Grices, and White; but they all withdrew into middle distance. Even Coleridge becomes after 1800 a factor of secondary importance and magnitude in the home-life of Lamb, precious beyond comparison as that mighty intellectual spirit once had been.

Lamb was continually gaining new friends and new correspondents. Of these the majority is represented, so far as our existing intelligence goes, by a letter or two; but in other cases the fresh names made their way to the front, and absorbed a leading share of attention for a season. From 1796 to 1798 all the letters are to Coleridge; during 1798 and 1799 they are divided between Southey and Manning; in 1800 Wordsworth and Godwin compete for a share.

In 1803 (or earlier), the Hazlitts appear on the scene, and continue to occupy during several years the leisure time of both the Lambs, the society of Hazlitt himself indemnifying Elia for the temporary loss of Manning. From 1807 to 1813 or 1814 there are few letters to anybody; it is the dark period, during which Lamb appears to have produced those till of late scarcely known literary trifles, *Beauty and the Beast*, *Prince Dorus*, and perhaps others yet to be identified. Between those years Canon Ainger has no more than five-and-twenty letters, of which three are to fresh and occasional correspondents, and the remainder to Coleridge, the Wordsworths, Manning, Godwin, and the Hazlitts. 1804, however, enjoys the unique distinction of having contributed only two items—the letters to Southey and Miss Stoddart.

From 1815 downward the supply is more abundant, and has a constant tendency to increase, since it was subsequently to the rise of a feeling that records of this character might possess enduring value, that some greater measure of care was taken to preserve them. But the old names are apt to recede into the background a little, and prominence is successively acquired by Alsop, Charles and John Chambers, Bernard Barton, Howard Payne and the Kenneys, Hone, Cowden Clarke and Novello, and Moxon.

It is for this reason, if there were no other, that it seems expedient and right to admit all that Lamb left behind him of an epistolary character without too nicely weighing its individual consequence. I do not believe that in his inmost heart the friends of his youth became less to him; but this intercourse on paper with more recent acquaintances constituted a valuable distraction, and more particularly after 1825, when his official duties determined, entered importantly into the business of every-day life. The modified calibre of the correspondence of later date may be gauged, to some extent, by the fact that in Canon Ainger's two volumes, Letters 1—162 fill 309 pages, while Letters 163—417 are comprised in 303. Two hundred and fifty-four letters, from 1817 to 1834, including the whole of the Barton series and others of not inconsiderable length, demand six pages fewer than the 162 letters of or prior to 1817.

I have quoted Lamb's own semi-serious saying, "that ever the new friend driveth out the old," but it was, of course, not entirely his own fault or even his own choice that the preponderance and personality of the letters fluctuated or varied from time to time. It might not be the truth, it perhaps scarcely ever was, that his own sentiment toward early friends faltered; but the movements of some of his intimates became uncertain, and, taking Manning as a sample, the absences of the *Missionary* from England or from Europe explain the paucity of communications during prolonged intervals. From 1799 to 1801 the flow was tolerably regular; then it began to slacken; in 1802—3 the breaks were wider; in 1804 there is nothing; in 1805—6, and more or less down to 1810, the series proceeded; then came a pause till 1815, another till 1819, and the correspondence is a blank between 1819 and 1825, and between the latter year and 1834. It was not invariably that Manning was abroad; the gaps are occasionally due to unpublished letters, occasionally to the fact that Lamb and he were in London together. But subsequently to 1829, it is stated that he lived in retirement at Bexley or elsewhere, and presumably forsook literary society and letter-writing, except as in the solitary item, to which Lamb responded in his of May 10, 1834, and in which we are invited to believe there was just the old vein of gaiety and humour. Possibly Manning did venture Londonward now and then, and put up at his friend Tuthill's in Cavendish Square.

A FEW BIOGRAPHICAL MEMORANDA

A FEW BIOGRAPHICAL MEMORANDA

WITH reference to the period during which the Lambs resided at Enfield Chase, I may mention that the late Mr. William Brailsford, who lived with his parents close by them, described to me how his mother was afraid of the brother and sister, and would not go near them, but that he had once spoken to Lamb. Mr. Brailsford also knew Coleridge and Hazlitt, and asked a common friend, before he met me, if I resembled my grandfather. He recalled in my hearing how, when he was at Harrow one speech-day, reading a book on some steps, a gentleman, passing, patted him on the shoulder, and made some remark in an under tone. It was Lord Byron.

When Lamb went to Enfield, he was probably unaware that he was the second person of that name who had fixed his abode in that locality. In 1707, a Charles Lamb was curate of the parish, and published one or two sermons. I do not know whether it is worth while to mention that a poem, entitled *Palengue, or the Ancient West*, by Charles Lamb, *Esquire*, appeared in 1849. This may be the Charles Lamb, Esq., who died at Chislehurst, Kent, September, 1890, aged 70.

Lamb, though he passed so much of his later years out of London, never formed any strong attachment to the scenery or pursuits of the country, and seldom refers to either. He was a good pedestrian; but his thoughts did not receive any colour from his rambles in the suburban lanes. His migrations from town to country were perhaps, however, serviceable as balancing distractions.

The point, on which I have insisted just above, as to Lamb's want and incapability of sympathy with rural scenery, is exemplified and confirmed in one of his latest letters—that to Manning in May, 1834, where he observes: "I walk 9 or 10 miles a day, always up the road, dear London-wards. Fields, flowers, birds, and green lanes, I have no heart for. The Ware road is cheerful, and *almost good as a street*. I saunter to the Red Lion daily, as you used to the Peacock."*

It is conceivable that the nervous stutter, to

* Comp. Canon Ainger's edition of the *Letters*, ii., 299.

which the utterance of Lamb was more or less subject, was favourable to the development of his pleasantries and *jeux-de-mot*. The delivery of the impromptu was colourably retarded by a natural impediment, for which no man could be entitled to blame the author. Of Lamb's quickness in repartee, however, there is no question; he seldom opened his lips in the course of friendly conversation without imparting some Attic salt to the dialogue; and of his sayings not a tithe has been published, and of such as have found their way into print the text is too often incorrect.

The history of the retirement from Leadenhall Street has never yet been quite clearly stated or understood. On the 7th of March, 1825, Lamb addressed a letter to the Company, setting forth that he had served as a clerk in the accountant's office for a period of nearly thirty-three years, and enclosing medical certificates of declining health, with a petition for leave to quit his office under the provisions of the Act 53 Geo. III., cap. 155. This letter was taken into consideration by the directors on the 16th, and referred to the committee of account. On the 29th the Board resolved to grant the applicant a pension for life of £450.

It further appears, from documents preserved at the India Office, that Lamb had contributed to the Regular Widows' Fund from its first establishment, April 1, 1816, till his death, a sum of £203. 19*s.* 1*d.*, in consideration of which the directors, on the 9th of March, 1835, resolved to settle on his sister, Mary Lamb, an annuity for her life of £120, she having already, under her brother's will, an income of £90 a year.

With these papers before me, there can be no objection to add that the original pay of Lamb was £40 a year, increased to £70 in 1796, and that his father had to become his surety in £500 on the 27th of April, 1792, twenty-two days after his appointment. On the 23rd of October, 1810, John Lamb having died in 1799, a fresh bondsman was required, perhaps on promotion, and was found in the person of James White, "of Warwick Square, newspaper agent"—the Jem White of the Life and Letters. William Savory, who is mentioned in the correspondence, received his nomination on the same day as his more illustrious colleague.

The nett quarterly payment from 1792 to 1796 appears to have been only £8. 15*s.* 7*d.*

Notwithstanding such slender resources and

the lapse of years before his salary became comfortably ample, Lamb is never found hinting at pecuniary difficulties, or at being in debt. He obeyed at all events one of Shakespear's precepts; but out of his moderate earnings he contrived to lend to his friends—more, probably, than we shall ever know—and saved a considerable amount, namely, the capital of the £90 a year just referred to.

The late Mr. Marmaduke Hornidge, of the India House, recollected Lamb coming there periodically for his pension. Mr. Ryle and Mr. Chambers were the two fellow clerks, of whom he saw most on these occasions. Lamb gave up, according to the ordinary rule and scale, two per cent. of his salary and pension to provide for his sister. The Company tacitly permitted the extension of the privilege, however, to any female relative domiciled with, and dependent on, a bachelor brother, or as the case might be, she receiving half the allowance granted to a widow.

In more than one conversation with Mr. Hornidge, I elicited without difficulty from him a candid avowal of his total inability to understand why people made such a fuss about an individual, whose official status was never very high, and who did not rise to the receipt of more than £600 a year. Mr. Hornidge was a Justice of the Peace for one of the divisions of Surrey, a gentleman of unblemished repute, and a foremost character in the parish of Barnes. *Requiescat in pace.*

Yet he was ostensibly a person of more than average density even for a public official, since others in the office, as Mr. Ryle, Mr. Chambers, Mr. Edward White, Mr. Brook Pulham (the Wither collector), and Mr. William Evans (the illustrator of Byron) for instance, were more or less awake to the companionship of a superior intellect in Lamb, and some of the members of the Board of Directors cannot have been wholly insensible to the fact. The "Bell Letters," as Elia more than once terms them, were very much indeed out of Mr. Hornidge's line.

There is an extant note to Ryle, which I print below with a feeling that I ought to apologise for its insignificance; but it is the only scrap with which I have met. There is a letter to White in my edition of the *Letters*. Of correspondence with Pulham and Evans I have no knowledge. It is, on the contrary, among the most satisfactory of recent discoveries, that with John Chambers, as well as his brother Charles,

Lamb exchanged communications; more particularly with the former.

Numerous references occur in the correspondence to the several portraits of Lamb himself taken at successive periods, and more or less recent publications offer a complete gallery of these supposed resemblances, commencing with the miniature, in which he appears as a young man of one and twenty or thereabout, executed in the hard, mechanical, and monotonous manner of Hancock. It is, perhaps, the least exceptionable of the set of four which that artist painted. Of the work by Hazlitt no adequate estimate can be formed from the engraving in Procter's book: but even when one contemplates the finished original in the National Portrait Gallery, the costume seems to detract from the effect. The painter was at the time (1805—6), when he was engaged in the task, fresh from the Louvre and its Titianesque associations, and was balancing between literature and art as a profession; and poor Lamb is arrayed in some nondescript trappings, intended to do duty for the dress of a Venetian senator.

The late Mr. Macmillan, the publisher, had an indifferent replica, purchased at an auction in 1880. I went to see it, before it was sold, but did not care to leave a commission. Yet it brought £60. That in the National Portrait Gallery was acquired at a cost of £105.

Looking at the whole assemblage of attempts to convey to posterity the lineaments and living expression of Lamb, I own that I prefer the likeness prefixed to the common edition of the Works, and next to that the one which accompanies Canon Ainger's book.

There is a story of Lamb illustrative of the saying that what goes in at one ear goes out at the other. Lamb was in a coach, and was accosted by the passenger next to him on one side, who suspected at last that he did not appreciate his remarks. "You do not appear," he said, "to be interested in my conversation?" Replies Lamb: "The gentleman next me has it."

A man, who had spent fifty years of his life in the Temple and neighbourhood, was asked by me whether he remembered the name of Lamb, *i.e.*, of course, Charles and Mary. He enquired whether this Lamb was in any way related to the Paschal Lamb. He had seen the cognizance over the Middle Temple door.

It is so usual to speak of Lamb's sister as Mary Lamb, that we lose sight of the fact that her full name was *Mary Ann Lamb*, as she writes it herself on the fly-leaf of a copy of her brother's works, which she gave to my father in 1842.

Lamb himself, in a receipt which he gave on her behalf in 1834, spells the second name *Anne*. Orthography was not a strong point with either of them; or rather they, like many others, had no settled standard.

LAMB'S LIBRARY

LAMB'S LIBRARY

A LIST of the books belonging to Lamb and his sister, and the greater part remarkable for interesting annotations by the former, has been already given in the volume published in 1874 by the present writer. Unfortunately he was precluded from seeing a proof of this portion; and the text is incorrect in several places. But it is also incómplete, and even the following items do not make up probably the sum of the "ragged regiment."

Beaumont and Fletcher. Comedies and Tragedies. Folio. 1647 or 1679. In the British Museum.

This has passed through the hands of Coleridge, who, in returning it to its owner, has written the following characteristic note:—"17th April, 1807. God bless you, dear Charles Lamb. I am dying; I feel I have not many weeks left." Singularly enough, in sending back a copy of Donne in 1811, the sombre persuasion that his end was near seems to have been still strong; for he inserts this memorandum:—"I shall die soon, my dear Charles Lamb, and then you will not be vexed that I have bescribbled your book." I print below the letter of 1808, in which the same sentence is repeated. Lamb evidently looked on these forebodings as semi-serious, or, at all events, hypochondriacal.

Burton (Robert). *Anatomy of Melancholy.* 4to. 1621. A very poor, cropped copy, with *Charles Lamb* on title, but the surname cut off by binder.

Daniel (Samuel). Poetical Works. 12mo. 1718. 2 vols. With two autograph letters by S. T. Coleridge on flyleaves, and numerous important notes, in the handwriting of Coleridge and Lamb, on margins.

Jonson (Benj.). Works. Folio. 1692.

He gave this book to Dr. Stoddart in 1803.

Browne (Sir Thomas, M.D.). Enquiries into Vulgar and Common Errors. Folio. 1658. With MSS. notes by S. T. Coleridge and the autograph of Lamb.

Holcroft (Thomas). Travels from Hamburgh, through Westphalia and the Netherlands, to Paris. 4to. 1804. 2 vols.

Lamb has made these volumes, flyleaves, margins and every other imaginable space, a receptacle for a variety of observations—has, in fact, turned them into a common-place book.

Milton (John). *Paradise Lost and Regained.* 8vo. 1751. 2 vols.

Imperfect, but with an assortment of critical notes, corrections, &c., by Lamb, throughout. In the British Museum.

Webster's *Duchess of Malfy*. The *Rehearsal*, by the Duke of Buckingham, and other Plays of the period or century by Wycherley, Etherege, Otway, &c., in a 4to. vol. With a list of the contents in Lamb's hand.

Gessner (S.). *Schriften.* 8vo. 3 vols. 1810. With the signature of Mary Lamb in each volume.

Donne (John). Paradoxes, Problems, Essays, Characters, &c. 12mo. 1652. With Lamb's autograph presentation to Isola:—"To dear Isola, 1834."

Shelley (P. B.). History of a Six Weeks' Tour through France, Switzerland, &c. 8vo. 1818. With Lamb's autograph on flyleaf.

Spenser (Edmund). Fairy Queen, Shepherd's Calendar, &c. Folio. 1612—17. With "M. Lamb, Alpha Road, No. 41." outside cover, and numerous MSS. notes by Lamb himself.

Tag, Rag, and Bob-Tail, a volume of modern miscellanies. 8vo. Forster Collection, South Kensington.

Talfourd (T. N.). Ion: a Tragedy. 8vo. No date. First Edition. Presentation copy from the author to Mary Lamb.

Taylor (Jeremy). Sermons. Folio. 1678. "C. Lamb, 1798," occurs on general title, and there are some MSS. notes by him, also one or two by S. T. Coleridge, one with his initials.

Warner (William). Syrinx; or, a Sevenfold History. 4to. 1597. Dyce Collection, South Kensington. Given to Lamb in 1823, with other books, by Harrison Ainsworth.

Wither (George). Poems. The Bristol reprint. 3 vols. Interleaved and bound in 2 vols, 4to., and filled with MSS. notes and criticisms by Lamb. This passed into the hands of Mr. A. C. Swinburne.

Miscellanies. Poems, by George Dyer, 1800. A Reply to Dr. Parr, by W. Godwin, 1801. The Speech of Lord Baron Fitzgibbon, 1793. 8vo. With MSS. notes by Lamb and Coleridge.

These books, with some others (including a few presented to William Hazlitt the younger by Miss Lamb, and restored to Moxon), remained in England, when the remainder was sold to Messrs. Welford and Scribner, of New York, and gradually dispersed. The late Mr. Charles Welford presented me, many years ago, with the subjoined particulars of the prices and purchasers' names, with the short titles of the articles. The figures realised were very handsome, and immeasurably above their commercial value at home at that time:—

Prices and Purchasers' Names of Sixty Volumes of Books, which belonged to Charles Lamb, sold in New York, February, 1848, *at Private Sale.*

NO.	WORK.	PURCHASER.	PRICE
1	Aulus Gellius	Bristed	$7·50
2	Art of Living, &c.	Annan of Cincinnatti, Ohio	2·50
3	Bourne, Vincent	Rev. Mr. Alexander	5·00
4	Burney, Jas.	Annan	1·50
5	Bacon, Lord	Woodman of Boston	4·00
6	Cities Great Concern	Annan	2·75
7	Cleveland's Poems	Balmanno	3·50
8	Ditto	Balmanno	4·00
9	Chaucer	Annan	25·00
10	Cowley	Woodman, Boston	10·00
11	The Dunciad	Livermore, Boston	3·50
12	Dennis	Jones	3·00
13	Drayton, Mich.	Annan	32·00
14	Euripides.	Norton, Boston	2·50
15	Edwards, Jonathan.	Livermore	3·50
16	Fulke Greville	Woodman	7·50
17	Guardian. Vol. I.	Folsom	5·00
18	Hudibras	Annan	3·00
19	Hymens Preludia	Annan	6·50
20	Ben Johnson	Strong	25·00
21	Lucans Pharsalia	Annan	2·50
22	More, Dr. Henry	Strong	8·00
23	Ditto	Deane, Boston	8 00
24	Ditto	Ditto	9·00
25	Minor Poets	Annan	3·00
26	Miscellanies	Strong	10·00
27	Miscellany Letters	Annan	5·00
28	Newcastle, Duchess of	Wetmore	12·00

NO.	WORK.	PURCHASER.	PRICE
29	Newcastle, Duchess of	Conant	10·00
30	Ditto	Cassiday, Louisville, Kentucky	9·00
31	Osborne, Francis	Folsom	3·50
32	Old Plays	Annan	10·00
33	Old Plays	Annan	10 00
34	Old Plays	Annan	9 00
35	Old Plays	A Stranger	12·00
36	Poetical Tracts	Annan	6·00
37	Ditto	Annan	6·00
38	Prior, Matthew	Balmanno	6·00
39	Plays	Bateman, Philadelphia	3·50
40	Philips, Mrs. K.	Annan	5·00
41	Relation, &c.	Ditto	1·50
42	Reliquiæ Wottonianæ	Wiley & Putnam, for Boston	5·00
43	Richardson, Mrs.	Richards	3·50
44	Review, &c.	Ditto	3·50
45	Shakspeare's Poems	Balmanno	6·00
46	Spectator Vol. IX.	Cassiday	1·50
47	Swift. Vol. V.	Balmanno	3·50
48	Suckling, Sir John	Woodman	5·00
49	Sewell, Wm.	Rev. H. W. Bellows.	12·00
50	Tryon, Thomas	Norton	3·00
51	Tale of a Tub	A Stranger	3·50
52	Tracts	Ditto	3·50
53	Ditto	Annan	5·50
54	Ditto	Annan	6·00
55	Waller's Poems	Balmanno	3·50
56	Buncle, John	Strong	8·50
57	Donne, Dr.	Strong	40·00
58	God's Revenge	Strong	30·00
59	Hist. P. de Comines	Strong	10·00
60	Pitvin, Rev. Mr.	Strong	20·00
			$479 75

Equal to £107. 18*s*. 11*d*.

It must be apparent to everyone that this enumeration does not embrace an assortment of modern contemporary literature, chiefly presentation copies from Southey, Wordsworth, Cottle, Barton, and other literary *confrères*. From allusions in the correspondence we perceive that not a year passed without the arrival at Lamb's fireside of tributes of prose and poetry, of all of which it became his duty to report the safe receipt and cordial appreciation. Critical estimates were sometimes solicited, and sometimes a review in an organ to which the recipient had access. These were rather painful accessories, where Lamb found a difficulty in saying or writing what was likely to satisfy the author, or, if the opinion was for publication, the editor and the public.

THE RARER ELIANA

THE RARER ELIANA

I HAVE no intention in the present case to come forward as a bibliographer. But I cannot resist the temptation of supplying a few new points, as they seem to me to be, in the history of the *Tales from Shakespear* and other early works. This popular little book, after passing through two editions in 1807 and 1808, reached a third in 1809, Godwin being still the publisher; but in the Preface to this issue it is explained that the book is printed in a superior style for the benefit of older readers, and that the plates given in the previous impressions have been withdrawn, a portrait of the author (Shakespear) being substituted. A few copies of the Blake prints, however, had been worked off, it is added, to suit those who liked such embellishments. On the back of the title is an extract from the *Critical Review* for May, 1807, recommending the book as the best of its kind, except *Robinson Crusoe*.

Rosamund Gray, Lamb's earliest separate production, appeared long before the *Tales*—that is to say, in 1798. The Lloyd influence had perhaps something to do with the issue of the book in the same year with a Birmingham imprint.

Let me now proceed to furnish the full particulars of two or three works (so to speak) of Lamb unknown to all his early biographers—namely, *Poetry for Children*, *Beauty and the Beast*, and *Prince Dorus*.

1. *Poetry for Children.* Entirely original. By the author of "Mrs. Leicester's School." In two volumes. London: Printed for M. J. Godwin, at the Juvenile Library, No. 41, Skinner Street. 1809. Sm. 8vo. Vol. I.: Frontispiece, 1 leaf, title and contents, pp. 4; the book, 104 pp. Vol. II., the same.
Sotheby's, Nov. 12, 1888, No. 407.

This little book, of which a great deal too much has been made by accidental possessors and by *dilettanti*, is really a very poor performance, as well as a palpable and weak imitation of similar child's poetry by the Taylors and others. "Little Ann" is earlier and better. The Lamb book was reprinted at Boston, N.E., 1812. Sm. 8vo., pp. 144.

2. *Beauty and the Beast; or, The Enchanted Rose.* A Poetical Version of an Ancient Tale. Illustrated

with a series of engravings; and Beauty's Song at her Spinning-wheel, set to music by Mr. Whittaker. Second edition. London: William Jackson & Co., at the Juvenile Library, 195 (St. Clement's) Strand. 1825. Three shillings plain; five shillings coloured. Sm. 8vo.

The first edition, I presume, was that described in an auctioneer's catalogue for December 18, 1885, as commencing, like the only other copy known, with the text, and as having coloured plates. The conjectured date was 1811, and the publisher, doubtless, was Godwin: Jackson and Co. having probably bought the stock after Godwin's failure.

3. *Prince Dorus; or, Flattery put out of Countenance.* A Poetical Version of an Ancient Tale. Illustrated with a series of elegant engravings. London: Printed for M. J. Godwin, at the Juvenile Library, No. 41, Skinner Street. 1811. Duodecimo, pp. 32, the last blank. In rhyming couplets.

Sotheby's, Feb. 14, 1888. The plates coloured. They are nine in number, and are attributed to Blake. There is no introductory matter, and no mention of the author. There was a second issue, 12mo., 1818, with coloured plates.

But a singular question arises here in connection with this particular copy of the last-named trifle. With it were bracketed two or three other similar productions, one being entitled

The Hare and many Friends, 1808, with coloured engravings. We all remember the *jeu d'esprit* of Lamb, where a friend invites him to dinner, and mentions that he has a hare for him. "And many friends?" inquires the proposed guest. From 1808 to 1812, or thereabout, forms a very ill-dated epoch in Lamb's career; the correspondence is almost a blank. Did he also write this child's book? I am sorry that I did not see it.

There is a point which merits a passing notice, and it is that the brother and sister's joint production, *Mrs. Leicester's School*, first published in 1809, and merely interesting to us as exhibiting several autobiographical hints, probably owed its title to a small juvenile book brought out by Newbery in 1794: *The Two Cousins: a Moral Story of Mrs. Leyster, for Young Persons.* Nothing is more likely than that such a volume fell in the way of the Lambs in early days.

The "Susan Yates" of this pretty and touching little book perhaps recalls the Timothy Yeats, Esq., who presented Lamb to Christ's Hospital in 1782. Had he a daughter Susan? It was twenty-seven years ago.

This book received the unique distinction of

being translated into French under the title of *Les Jeunes Pensionnaires*, 12mo., Paris, 1824.

Lamb in nearly everything which he committed to paper—is it not the same with all of us?—had some actual substratum of fact behind him, some nucleus, which he elaborated, and perhaps disguised on personal or other grounds. The late Professor Morley even went so far as to allege at a venture that the names of the Benchers of the Inner Temple, set forth in the Elian essay on that subject, were fictitious, although he might have been warned by the presence on the list of Samuel Salt, the patron of Lamb's father. The only liberty which the author of the paper has really taken is in the case of Mr. Twopeny; and even he was a student of the Inn, as appears from the Register. Among the portraits preserved by the Inn of its former worthies is one of "Mingay with the Iron Hand." This was James Mingay, admitted in 1770, called to the Bench in 1785, and Treasurer in 1791. He died in 1812. He had lost a hand, and is represented with a hook as a substitute for it.

In the *London Magazine* for January, 1822, we come across *A Dramatic Fragment*, with the mysterious signature * * * at the end. But it is known to be Lamb's, and Sir Theodore

Martin once lent me the original MS. It is the familiar story of the author's "fair-haired maid" in a dramatic shape—a mere little sketch, occupying two-thirds of a page of the magazine. It is to this episode, of which an actual passage of his very early life was beyond doubt the groundwork, that he alludes in a sonnet enclosed with his letter to Coleridge of (June) 1796:—

"When last I roved these winding wood-walks green,
Green winding walks and shady pathways sweet,
Oft-times would Anna seek the silent scene."

This was, perhaps, his first boyish fancy. The dramatist seems to convey that the blonde damsel, unlike her nut-brown ancestor, proved unkind and untrue. Who can say?

The clues given in my Lamb volume of 1874 evidently set Canon Ainger on the track of Bartrum the pawnbroker, and he procured, I understand, through Mr. Harrison of the London Library, an introduction to the representative of that family, associated in an earlier generation with the essayist's youthful love affair. It has hitherto, I believe, remained unsuggested that there may be some connection between the Alice W . . n mystery and Lamb's farce of *The Pawnbroker's Daughter*, contributed to *Blackwood* in 1830. I elsewhere* notice that William Coulson, the surgeon, married one of Bartrum's daughters.

But the *chef d'œuvre* of Lamb in his popular publications was the *Adventures of Ulysses*, a prose paraphrase of the *Odyssey*. I have repeatedly wept over it; but it may not be generally known that Godwin exercised a sort of readership here; for in a letter to him of March 11, 1808, the author thanks him for having pointed out the revolting description of Polyphemus devouring the companions of the hero, and notifies its removal; while he combats other objections *a l'outrance*, declaring that he will not alter the passages, even if Godwin and the rest of the trade should refuse the book on that account.

Under date of October 25, 1839, occurs the following in Caroline Fox's Journal:—"Soon after Fauntleroy was hanged, an advertisement appeared: 'To all good Christians! Pray for the soul of Fauntleroy.' This created a good deal of speculation as to whether he was a Catholic, and at one of Coleridge's *soirées* it was

* *Four Generations of a Literary Family*, 1897, i., 282.

discussed for a considerable time; at length Coleridge, turning to Lamb, asked: 'Do you know anything about this affair?' 'I should think I d-d-did,' said Elia, 'for I paid s-s-s-seven and sixpence for it.'"

The revolution in the prices of first editions of Lamb's writings would have struck their author more forcibly, perhaps, even than it strikes a contemporary observer. A few shillings would, some forty years ago, have placed one in possession of the whole series. There was a slight upward tendency within my recollection, however. I was in Mr. John Waller's shop in Fleet Street, and he offered me a beautiful copy, in sheep, of the *editio princeps* of the *Tales from Shakespear* (1807), for 7*s*. 6*d*., mentioning that Mr. George Daniel (who died in 1864) had been in, and had pronounced the book to be worth a guinea.

Mr. H., though a failure at the period of its original performance, was successfully revived in the author's life-time—about 1827, and again in 1885. A piece like this wholly depends on the person filling the principal part. Toole or Terry might, perhaps, make a hit with it. But it is so slight in its construction, that it is something like a jest dramatized.

The volume of Poems by Charles Lloyd, mentioned above (p. 27), is entitled: *Poems on the Death of Priscilla Farmer*, by her Grandson, Charles Lloyd. Bristol. Printed by N. Biggs, and sold by James Phillips, George Yard, Lombard Street, London, 1796. Folio, pp. 27. With a quotation on the title-page from Bowles.

This little work, for a description of which I am indebted to Mr. B. B. Macgeorge, of Glasgow (through Messrs. Pearson & Co., of Pall-Mall Place*), includes the poem by Lamb, entitled "The Grandam," which was reprinted with alterations in Coleridge's Poems, 12mo., 1797. In introducing it at p. 25, Lloyd says: "The following beautiful fragment was written by Charles Lamb, of the India House. Its subject being the same with that of my poems, I was solicitous to have it printed with them, and I am indebted to a Friend of the Author for the permission." These verses are of special interest as the earliest appearance of Lamb in type.

* In Mr. MacGeorge's copy there is the inscription by the poet (at that time his father was living): "Charles Lloyd, Jun., to his Uncle S. Galton. 1796."

OBSERVATIONS ON THE CORRESPONDENCE

OBSERVATIONS ON THE CORRESPONDENCE

THE interest of published letters is ordinarily held to depend either on the writer or the matter written. It is more difficult than may at first sight appear to decide which is the more attractive feature; but it is certain that, where the two are combined, we realise this class of writing in its perfection.

There are, doubtless, many epistolary relics of the Lambs, brother and sister, which are trivial enough, and which, had they proceeded from the pen of an obscure or uninteresting person, might be in danger of committal to the waste-basket, just as there are specimens of correspondence by inferior writers which are only redeemed from neglect because their merit is purely intrinsic.

The serious injustice done to the Hazlitt book of 1886 by its two years' junior, that of Canon Ainger, forms a subject on which the present writer feels a natural delicacy in dwelling or insisting too much in this place. He had, in the preparation of his own volumes, tried to exhaust every known or accessible channel and source of information, with a view to the farther recension of the text and the more approximate completeness of the series of letters.

He felt it to be out of the question to aspire or pretend to finality; but he took the longest step possible in the right and true direction. Numerous important additions were incorporated; every letter within reach was compared; and a large body of explanatory notes was supplied. He did his best, but he should have liked to have been enabled at that time to do better.

My undertaking was entitled, *Letters of Charles Lamb, with some Account of the Writer, His Friends and Correspondents, and Explanatory Notes.* By the late Sir Thomas Noon Talfourd, D.C.L., one of his Executors. An Entirely New Edition, Carefully Revised and Greatly Enlarged. By W. Carew Hazlitt. London, 1886, small 8vo. 2 vols. Vol. 1, pp. 451 and xl.; Vol. 2, pp. 477 and vi.

There was no particular reason, I believe, to complain of a want of success, and the popularity of the subject, which seems well nigh inexhaustible, assisted the sale of a large number of copies. But certain circumstances of a collateral nature occurred both before and subsequently to inspire me with a feeling of dissatisfaction, when I considered how peculiarly my name was identified, by inheritance and otherwise, with that of the Lambs. For, after all, who, during the last thirty years, before most of the existing editors were born, or at best heard of,* has exerted himself more assiduously and more loyally in improving the public knowledge in this direction?

Two years later, Canon Ainger, having succeeded in enlisting the services of several friends, and having been permitted access to certain papers unseen by his predecessor, brought out *The Letters of Charles Lamb Newly arranged, with Additions.* London, 1888, small 8vo. 2 vols. Vol. 1, pp. 343 and xxviii; vol. 2, pp. 377 and xiv.

Never, in the entire compass of modern literary history, has a gentleman been so phenomenally unfortunate as this deponent has been in his Elian labours.

* My earliest Lamb essay was in the shape of a paper in *Macmillan's Magazine* in 1866.

Imprimis, his collected edition, of which the first volume appeared in 1868, came out without his name at the outset, and then with several members of the alphabet in succession, according to the caprice of the tricksy publisher.

Secundo, the late Mrs. Anne Gilchrist, having honoured him by a request for leave to make use of his "Mary and Charles Lamb," 1874, signalized her appreciation of its contents by grounding her own book entirely upon it.

Here is Mrs. Gilchrist's letter to me *exempli gratiâ*:

"Keats' Corner,
"Well Road, Hampstead.
"Nov. 9, 82.

"Dear Sir,—Will you kindly permit me to print Mary Lamb's letters to Mrs. Hazlitt in my forthcoming Life of Mary? They contribute so important a part of our knowledge of her, and are, in fact, so completely *Mary herself*, that a biographer would be in sad straits were he denied the privilege of incorporating them.

Do you know when Thomas Manning died? If he survived Lamb, I wonder why there are no letters to him during the last ten years of his life—nor does he seem to have been at the funeral.

"I am, dear sir,
"Yours faithfully,
"ANNE GILCHRIST."

Tertio comes Canon Ainger, who wins praise on all sides for reproducing, with some additions (and many omissions), in 1888, what this deponent printed in 1886, the substance and arrangement being identical, with the exception of the Talfourd gloss.

All that was required to complete the process was an acknowledgment. Is your servant a jackal, that men (and women, marry, too) should thus entreat him? Is he but a bush-beater?

I have, of late years, accomplished much in the direction alike of rehabilitating the text of known letters of Lamb and his sister, by the insertion of suppressed passages and the removal of faulty readings, and by the formation of quite a series of unpublished correspondence, bringing us to the conclusion that rarely a day passed without the post receiving some communication or other destined for an old or a new acquaintance.

These documents are almost invariably on one side, since Lamb, with half-a-dozen exceptions, destroyed all papers which came into his possession—not only such as perished under the influence of some momentary frenzy or hypochondriacal fit, but absolutely everything. Of course he did not stand alone in a dislike to the sight of old letters; but, in his case, the not uncommon feeling was intensified by their association with early troubles and bygone sorrows.

The Lamb correspondence stands on an unique basis, when we consider its extent, its importance and the long series of years over which it extends. Strictly speaking, it is not a correspondence at all; for we have, with a very limited number of exceptions, merely the letters addressed by the writer to his friends and others, while those received by him have perished by the hand, not of undiscerning or too fastidious representatives, but of the recipient himself at or near the time.

The accepted notion is, that under the influence of the profound sorrow and depression occasioned by his mother's melancholy death, he destroyed all the letters which he had had from Coleridge, and formed a resolution thenceforth to preserve nothing else of the sort. But, whether such be or be not the case, the main fact at all events is clear enough, and we are compelled to infer what the topic and nature of the communications made to the Lambs were from the tenor of the replies.

The loss of the invaluable assemblage of epistolary monuments once in the hands of Lamb and his sister is ascribable to an impulse, which was as disastrous and deplorable as it was obviously unhealthy or morbid. Yet it is possible to comprehend how, in the depth of the mental distress and despondency which attended and followed the death of his mother, and the pronounced insanity of his sister, Lamb may have wildly imagined that it was better to cast away all clues and ties tending to recall, or bring into distincter prominence, the dismal tragedy and its sequel.

There must have been moments when he repented of what he had done, and, as I have suggested, he consigned to the flames everything which came to his hands, as soon as it was read and answered, that the fruits of a mad spasm might be invested with a n aspect of consistency and design.

At first sight we do not attain an exhaustive conception of the harm done by the garbling and expurgating processes; for we by no means instantaneously realise how far superior a facility must always exist for mutilating the text of autograph letters dispersed among a large number of owners by inheritance or purchase, not only in the country of their production but abroad, to that for restoring it to its full proportions and integrity.

Every variety of impediment is thrown in the path of the editor who endeavours to do justice to his author and to the public at large. The MSS. are in the hands of jealous amateurs, of severe moralists, or such as have severe moralists at their elbow; of folks whose whereabouts are unknown, or perhaps of dealers, who refuse the privilege of inspection on commercial grounds. In other words, the longer the opportunities for collating Lamb MSS. with the printed copies are neglected by those who are superior to foolish scruples, the more complex and doubtful becomes the task of presenting to readers this splendid heritage in its unshorn plenitude.

The position is at present complicated by the natural perplexity of those who are repeatedly asked for the use of the same MSS. by different editors, and who are not readily satisfied that those, who have gone before, have not taken full advantage of their opportunity. In the Notes here and there one, on second thought, adds a few items, a passage or two, or whatever it may be, which ought to have formed part of the text, and might very well have done so, as the matter was before him in the first instance.

The extension of a pruning hand to his correspondence might not have surprised Lamb so greatly as the notion that it was deemed worthy of survival in a printed shape. Had such a thing been possible, only one other spectacle—I mean the fact that his own works and his sister's occupy nearly five-and-twenty pages of the British Museum Catalogue—could have inspired the author with more profound astonishment and even dismay, than the production of his written conversations with his friends, to which a fair proportion of the letters amount, in type for universal currency and instruction.

But the feature about them in their transformed condition, which would have most forcibly struck him, would have been the theory that a considerable number of passages required castration in order to satisfy the public sense of decorum. In one of his later communications he humourously refers to having unexpectedly lived to grow into "an indecent character;" but he never seriously dreamed that his correspondence would undergo two *inquisitiones post mortem.*

We have only to wait to see Walpole, Sterne, Voltaire, Pepys, and all the rest, reformed *secundum usum Christianum*, or, rather, denaturalized, in order to pander to a morbid effeminacy of taste.

Canon Ainger is sanguine, indeed, where he remarks in his Introduction: "Material for a final collection of Lamb's letters has been gradually accumulating since the appearance of Talfourd's well-known volumes"—sanguine, that is to say, if he looks on his own edition or any other hitherto in the market as answering to such a description or requirement.

The access to the Manning and Barton papers was a stroke of good fortune, for which I feel grateful in the public interest, and the letters to Dodwell, Dibdin, and Chambers are desirable accessions. But, after all, the bulk of Canon Ainger's volumes is not fresh, and the remainder is only a further quota, in common with much in my own, toward the *really* final collection of the letters—whenever that may be attempted or become feasible.

The expression on the title-page, "Newly arranged with additions," might perhaps lead the reader or student to conclude that the method there followed is new, and that, while there are supplementary items, the whole of the matter in former editions is incorporated. Such is, however, not the case, and the withdrawal or suppression of certain portions of the correspondence by the Canon cannot always be justified on the score of insignificance, though it may have been prompted by delicacy. Yet we must note that in other instances the Canon has freely adopted the Hazlitt text, just as he has done the Hazlitt arrangement.

These are points of detail. The main consideration is, that neither the Ainger nor the Hazlitt book is all that we want. Very far from it indeed; for the two negatives, so to say, would scarcely make an affirmative!

The two are before the reading public, and are more or less capable of telling their own story.

The matter still required to complete even the sequence of such letters as are already in type is susceptible of a distribution into two categories: 1, those which are hopelessly lost; 2, those which are probably recoverable.

The vitally important character and great extent, by fair inference, of the former division throw into the shade all the possibilities likely to arise under the second head. Let me enumerate. There are seemingly beyond redemption:

1. The entire correspondence with John Lamb.
2. " " " Fenwick.
3. " " " Tuthill.
4. " " " "the rich relation."

5. Commencement of correspondence with Coleridge.
6. " " " Southey.
7. " " " Manning (?).
8. " " " Wordsworth.
9. " " " Hazlitt & Stoddart.
10. " " " Mrs. Williams.
11. Portions of correspondence with Charles Lloyd and his wife.
12. " " " Charles Chambers.
13. " " " John Chambers.
14. " " " George Dyer.
15. " " " William Godwin.
16. " " " B. W. Procter.
17. " " " W. H. Ainsworth.
18. Later letters to W. Hazlitt.

It was by the purest miracle that the surviving letters to the Hazlitts were saved from a similar fate. By a singular, yet common, obliquity of reasoning, the majority of people argue that the moment a distinguished connection has ceased to breathe, his papers ought to share his lot, whereas the fact is exactly the reverse.

The unprinted matter divides itself into what is in all appearance irrecoverable, and what has not yet come into the hands of an editor. In the latter category may be comprised:—

1. Letters to Coleridge after 1796.
2. " Rickman.
3. " the Bethams.
4. " the Stoddarts.

5. Letters to the Kenneys.
6. " Colleagues at the India House. John Chambers and others.
7. A letter to Annette Lane, the actress.
8. " Miss Humphreys.
9. Letters to other members of the Chambers family.

Nos. 1, 2, 7, and 8 are almost certainly in existence, and the same is believed to be the case with the letters to Charles and John Chambers, of each of which series only a single item has so far been published.

The eighteenth century letters to Coleridge, from 1796 to 1800, always struck me as imperfectly presented in the editions; and since the issue of Canon Ainger's and my own I have had the opportunity of verifying my surmise, and supplying the *lacunæ*.

A thorough collation, not only of the Coleridge, but of the Wordsworth and Manning series, is, as the late Mr. Dykes Campbell said to me, imperative.

From a thoughtful survey of this schedule, some notion may be derived of what the correspondence might have been, if it had been preserved in its fullest integrity; and, again, how splendidly different it would have appeared, even supposing that every extant letter had been forthcoming in its true unsophisticated proportions. But between the latter alternative and the best, which has heretofore been accomplished, there is *longum intervallum.*

I may, perchance, find myself fortunate enough to secure a fair share of support in my contention and belief that Lamb was, above all, a Letter-Writer. Our estimation of him would be very much the same, if he had not given us anything but his correspondence.

His poetical and dramatic trifles amount, of course, to very little indeed. *Mr. H.* is scarcely more than a joke theatrically formulated; and, except the *Extracts from the Garrick Plays*, there is really nothing which might not have been embodied in an epistle to Coleridge, or to Manning, or to Barton.

There are letters upon letters, capable of being particularized, at least as fine, as wise, as witty, and (save the mark!) as pure as any Elian paper, while it would not prove a very difficult task to throw the two series, and all the other writings of that nature, into the epistolary form without substantial damage.

If it be true, then, that the correspondence is the central point of interest and consequence, the duty grows all the more onerous and responsible of establishing a standard text, and arriving as soon as possible at completeness of material.

I affirm that the admirers of Lamb on both sides of the Atlantic ask for the means of judging for themselves exactly on the same principle as the movement now in progress for giving us at last, after a terrible struggle, the *Diary of Pepys*, with the fewest possible exceptions, just as Pepys left it to posterity. Numerous enough, to be sure, are the dry, dispensable entries; but let us have the whole—prythee, let us not be dependent on individual or temporary sentiment.

The best plan to conceal an objectionable feature is to say nothing about it, not, if it is an engraving, to put it in a pocket at the end of the volume, or if it is letterpress, to relegate it to an appendix, as Dr. Furnivall did with the "Loose and Humorous Ballads" in the *Percy Folio MS*.

In the letter to Manning (Ainger, No. 79), where, in speaking of the powerful and enduring impression made upon him by some hostile criticism, he employs an honest Saxon word totally unsuitable for the ear polite, Talfourd, to compromise the matter, and let everyone understand that he has ventured upon a genteeler phrase, *prints the substitute in italics*. "My *back*," Lamb is made to write, "tingles from the northern castigation." The oddest case of this sort, however, is where, in a note to Moxon, of August, 1833, Lamb himself mistook the drift and terms of the once popular metaphor, "An ass in a bandbox."

In the letter to Coleridge of September 8, 1802, a vital passage, of which the suppression even by Talfourd is barely intelligible, seeing that Lloyd died long before 1848, is omitted by the more recent editors. It runs as follows: "Lloyd has written me a fine letter of friendship, all about himself and Sophia, and love, and cant, which I have not answered. I have not given up the idea of writing to him, but it will be done very plainly and sincerely, without acrimony."

The omissions in the letter to Manning of February 26, 1808, are rather serious (Hazlitt, i., 388; Ainger, i., 243). After "sinful" we ought to read: "*Splendida vitia* at best. Stay, while I remember it, Mrs. Holcroft was safely delivered of a girl some day in last week. Mother and child doing well. Mr. Holcroft has been attacked with a severe rheumatism. They have removed to Clipstone Street." And on the next page, after "something like that," Lamb wrote: "Godwin keeps a shop in Skinner Street, Snow Hill; he is turned children's bookseller, and sells penny, twopenny, threepenny, and fourpenny books. Sometimes he gets an order for the dearer sort of books. (Mind, all that I tell you in this letter is true.)" Finally, the Latin quotation just below should be, *Pauper est Cinna tamen sed amat.*

In the letters to William Godwin, of which both the writer and Canon Ainger had the use, by favour of Mr. Kegan Paul, it so happened that, the former being first in the field, he was not apprised, till it was too late, that three serious misprints had been overlooked by the biographer of Godwin in seeing his volumes through the press, and had been of course transferred to his own pages. Two occur in letters given both by Ainger and Hazlitt, but the remaining one is in an extract given by Kegan Paul as the only portion of a piece of the correspondence referring to Godwin's *Antonio*, in his judgment worthy of preservation. The word *beg*, near the end, was substituted for *lug*.

To William Godwin.

[A portion of a letter.]

[1800.]

"Enviable" is a very bad word. I allude to "enviable right to bless us." For instance, Burns, comparing the ills of manhood with the state of infancy, says, "Oh! enviable early days; here 'tis good, because the passion lay in comparison. Excuse my insulting your judgment with an illustration. I believe I only wanted to lug in the name of a favourite Bardie, or at most to confirm my own judgment."

These and such like are what are technically denominated "literals," and under the same head must be classed a slip of the pen in a letter to Hazlitt of 1826, of which the history is rather curious. It was a stray from the family collection, and was accidentally recovered shortly before the appearance of the volumes issued by Messrs. Bell in 1886. The text was derived from a transcript in a not too legible hand, and two inaccuracies in it were only detected when, by an afterthought, a *fac-simile* of the document was inserted as a specimen of Lamb's writing, and a collation of the two revealed the unfortunate inadvertence. Never was so striking an instance known before of an unhappy editor standing for ever self-convicted—"hoisted by his own petard." There, surely enough, are the type and the lithograph face to face! On the other hand, in a letter to Manning not given by me, I observe at a cursory glance that Canon Ainger, just at the end, prints for "Ware road daily," *bare road duly*.

As an illustration of the liability of editors to be misled, where the dependence is on an indistinct postmark or on a secondary authority, the letter sent by Lamb to John Taylor from Margate in 1821, respecting a proposed paper on Midsummer-Day for the *London Magazine*, proves a salient piece of evidence. In the Hazlitt book it is cited as written July 8, 1831, and in Ainger as belonging to June 8, same year, whereas the true note of time is June 8, 1821. Internal evidence shews that it was written in June, that it was prior to 1825, when the writer retired from the India House, and that it was in existence while the *London Magazine* still survived. It is due to Ainger to add that, while he ranges it under 1831, he intimates in his notes a suspicion that it properly forms part of the correspondence of a decade before.

Lamb left his friends very frequently to rely on the postmark or on internal testimony for the chronology of his notes to them, and this course was attended by a degree of inconvenience at and near the period of dispatch not comparable with that which it produces after the lapse of many years and the death of all immediately concerned. Sometimes, as if to illustrate the principle that the exception proves the rule, Lamb was almost ostentatiously elaborate in his indications, as in the letter to Bernard Barton of July 25, 1829, where he excuses the customary omission of such particulars on the plea that since his superannuation he had nothing to do with time:—

> "What have I with time to do?
> Slaves of desks, 'twas meant for you."

Yet he is, perhaps, equally remiss prior to his retirement.

In the Ainger volumes occur three consecutive letters to Joseph Cottle, of Bristol (Nos. 177-8-9). They are dated respectively [1819], [1819], and November 5, 1819.

The first states that Lamb had not seen or heard so long of Cottle, that he was ashamed to apply to him for a favour, which, however, he did by soliciting for a friend (and colleague at the India House, Mr. William Evans) a portrait of Cottle, for the purpose—as the Canon was the first to discover—of having it reproduced to illustrate the copy of Byron's *English Bards and*

Scotch Reviewers, then the property of Mr. Evans, and at present in the British Museum.

These letters were originally printed by Cottle in his *Recollections of Coleridge*, 1837, and are reprinted in the book as reissued in 1847. Cottle furnishes no dates to the first and second (Nos. 177-8 of Ainger), but implies that they were written in 1819. I have referred to the purport of the first; the second reports the execution of the copy of Cottle's likeness by a daughter of Josephs, A.R.A., the intended restitution of the original, and the receipt of a copy of Cottle's *Messiah*, on which Lamb offers certain criticisms.

So far, so good. But the remaining communication offers a difficulty. Cottle himself dates it: "London, India House, May 26, 1829." The year is undoubtedly wrong; for a glance will shew that it was written at the India House before 1825. The Canon gives November 5, 1819, as the true point of time; but the letter applying for the loan of the portrait bears date in the autograph MS. November 5, 1819, although the third figure of the year might easily be mistaken, as it was by me in my *Mary and Charles Lamb*, 1874, and in the 1886 volumes, for a 2. The Ainger sequence seems to be correct; but whence did the reverend editor derive his authority for dating No. 179 November 5? The first was written on that day, and there must have been an interval of many weeks between 177 and 179 of the Canon's collection. It is a case in which nobody is exactly right, and everyone somehow rather wrong. But the context must be allowed to govern the order, the discrepancies as to the dates or supposed dates being subject to rectification on that basis. The Hazlitt book, owing to the misreading by the editor of the original MS., unfortunately lets the item, which should be the last of the triad, fall altogether out of its natural succession. The tiresome result, is that three items in the series, which are closely connected together, have been separated by a whole decade, and that all sorts of halting conclusions have been formed about the circumstances. Next time the present writer will not trust even his very author; for the Canon has capitalized the blunder, and proclaimed its enormity from the house-top. In truth, he has slightly exceeded the fact; for in the Hazlitt book one of the trio is in its right place, and I also see that all are more accurately presented in Hazlitt than in Ainger, especially the last, of which the Ainger text is very unsatisfactory. He did not resort to the originals nor to his immediate precursor.

But I have not yet quite done with the Chambers affair. I discern in the letter, as printed by Canon Ainger, a vein of pleasant exaggeration and one or two hoaxes interspersed; but the whole, no doubt, is substantially true, and not "a tissue of audacious invention and wildest humour," or the "simplest romance," as the Canon thinks and writes. We are all perfectly aware that Lamb was prone to facetious outrages on veracity, which he usually avowed and retracted in a later communication. The prevalent superstition as to an inevitable underplot in every serious statement made by a man, who had gained notoriety as a humourist, seems to be at the bottom of this mischief. The Canon would have treated as a grim or quaint joke a note from Grimaldi, purporting to have been sent from a bed of sickness, or from Liston, complaining of hypochondria. Lamb "embellishes" a little, and it is all wild humour and romance!

A more egregious example, however, is afforded by the letter to Procter of January 19th, 1829, about the Dowden business, which Talfourd appears to have treated with his customary negligence and *laisser aller* indifference at a jest pure and simple. The Canon considers that the outline of the statement is veracious, but all the explanatory technicalities "the wildest romance."

I contend, on the contrary, that the view taken by me in 1886 is the correct one, and that Lamb was thoroughly serious throughout. The affair cost him a vast amount of worry and sleeplessness, and engrossed a good deal of time. Upward of a twelvemonth later, in a letter to Louisa Martin (July 11th, 1830), he says explicitly:—"I am engaged all over with Mrs. Dowden, my niece, who has come from Brighton on business very pressing to her." It is high time that this ostensible misrepresentation about Lamb's "wild humour" was discontinued. Of his real wit and fun we can never have a surfeit.

The true letter-hunter is constantly multiplying his experiences alike in the direction of triumph and failure. In the Hazlitt book of 1886, the editor, in a footnote to the letter to Bernard Barton, of July 10th, 1823, in which Lamb describes his impressions of Hastings, imagined himself on the track of a second allusion to the same place, having in fact mistaken an extract from the Elian paper on the *Old Margate Hoy* for one from a communication to some friend. The for the moment prevailing cue was the source of deception; the only comfort is that there is one lost or strayed letter the less to seek or to regret.

The Canon by no means stands alone in taking the public into his confidence by requiring them to receive his judgment on trust. The editor of the correspondence of Leigh Hunt prints an extract from a letter sent to Hunt by Lamb, in recognition of a presentation copy of the *Story of Rimini*. It is apparently the earliest communication between the two schoolfellows, yet we are to content ourselves with a bit of it, and on personal inquiry many years since I was informed that the Hunt family knew nothing about the original. It was probably extant in 1860, when the Letters of Hunt were published by his son. What has become of it? This form of vandalism is deplorable.

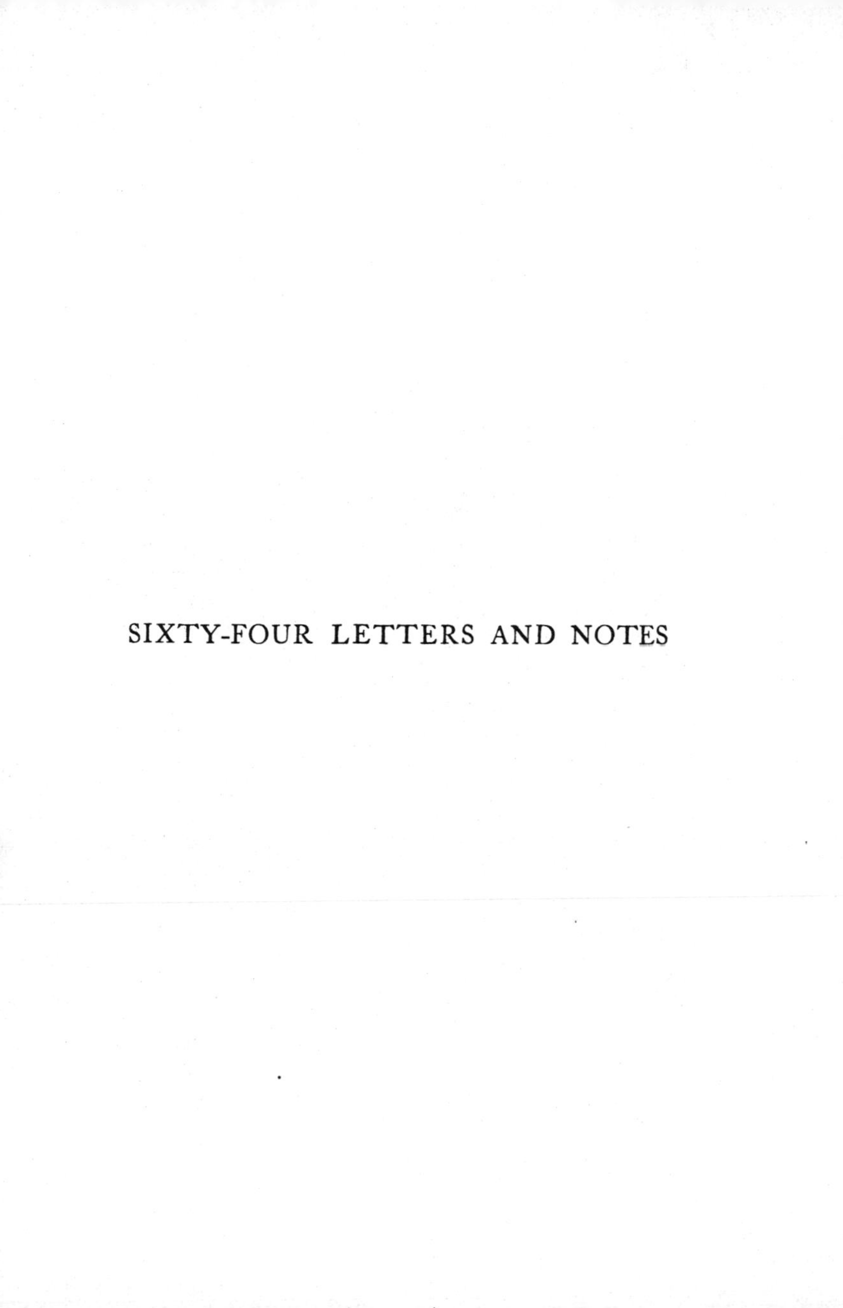

SIXTY-FOUR LETTERS AND NOTES

SIXTY-FOUR LETTERS AND NOTES

I HAVE now the pleasure of laying before the reader a long series of letters of the brother and sister, many of which are here first printed, while very few are in the editions by Canon Ainger and myself. It was deemed, on the whole, better to group the whole of this body of matter together, and to distinguish letters which have been given on former occasions, imperfectly or inaccurately, by an asterisk. Without receiving into account the slight textual divergences from the following letters to Coleridge as given by the two latest editors, a considerable portion is altogether omitted by both in common, of course, with all their predecessors. In the second letter we have hitherto missed the important reference to Godwin and the description of his movements, not long prior to the unsuccessful production of *Antonio*. Lamb generously desired to afford the author of *Political Justice* an opportunity of extending his acquaintance among the circle at the Lakes. Coleridge he already knew.

I*

"*To S. T. Coleridge.*[1]

["Little Queen Street, Night of December 9, 1796. Postmarked December 10, 1796.]

"I am sorry I cannot now relish your poetical present[2] as thoroughly as I feel it deserves; but I do not the less thank Lloyd and you for it. In truth, Coleridge, I am perplexed, and at times almost cast down. I am beset with perplexities. The old hag of a wealthy relation, who took my aunt off our hands in the beginning of trouble, has found out that she is 'indolent and mulish'—I quote her own words, and that her attachment to us is so strong, that she can never be happy apart. The Lady, with delicate Irony, remarks that, if I am not an Hypocrite, I shall rejoyce to receive her again, and that it will be a means of making me more fond of home to have so dear a friend to come home to! The fact is she is jealous of my aunt's bestowing any kind recollections on us, while she enjoys the patronage of her roof. She says she finds it inconsistent with her own 'ease and tranquility' to keep her any longer, and in fine summons me to fetch her home. Now, much as I should rejoyce to transplant the poor old creature from the chilling air

[1] From the original autograph.

[2] Poems. By S. T. Coleridge. Second Edition. To which are now added Poems by Charles Lloyd and Charles Lamb, 1797.

of such patronage, yet I know how straitened we are already, how unable already to answer any demand, which sickness or any extraordinary expence may make. I know this, and all unused as I am to struggle with perplexities, I am somewhat nonplusd, to say no worse. This prevents me from a thorough relish of what Lloyd's kindness and yours have furnished me with. I thank you tho from my heart, and feel myself not quite alone in the earth.

"Before I offer, what alone I have to offer, a few obvious remarks on the poems you sent me, I can but notice the odd coincidence of two young men, in one age, carolling their grandmothers. Love,—what L[loyd] calls 'the feverish and romantic tye,' hath too long domineerd over all the charities of home: the dear domestic tyes of father, brother, husband. The amiable and benevolent Cowper has a beautiful passage in his *Task*,—some natural and painful reflections on his deceased parents: and Hayley's sweet lines to his mother are notoriously the best things he ever wrote. Cowper's lines[1] some of them are—

> 'How gladly would the man recall to life
> The boy's neglected sire; a mother, too,
> That softer name, perhaps more gladly still,
> Might he demand them at the gates of death.'

I cannot but wish to see my Granny so gayly deck'd forth, tho', I think, whoever altered 'thy' praises to 'her' praises—'thy' honoured memory to 'her' honoured memory, did wrong—they best exprest my feelings. There is a pensive state of

[1] *Winter Walk at Noon.*

recollection, in which the mind is disposed to apostrophise the departed objects of its attachment; and breaking loose from grammatical precision, changes from the 1st to the 3rd, and from the 3rd to the 1st person, just as the random fancy or feeling directs. Among Lloyd's sonnets, 6th, 7th, 8th, 9th, and 11th are eminently beautiful. I think him too lavish of his expletives; the *dos* and *dids*, when they occur too often, bring a quaintness with them along with their simplicity, or rather air of antiquity, which the patrons of them seem desirous of conveying.

"The lines on Friday are very pleasing—'Yet calls itself in pride of Infancy woman or man,' &c., 'affection's tottering troop'—are prominent beauties. Another time, when my mind were more at ease, I could be more particular in my remarks, and I would postpone them now, only I want some diversion of mind. The *Melancholy Man* is a charming piece of poetry, only the 'whys' with submission are too many. Yet the questions are too good to be any of 'em omitted. For those lines of yours, page 18, omitted in magazine, I think the 3 first better retain'd—the 3 last, which are somewhat simple in the most affronting sense of the word, better omitted—to this my taste directs me—I have no claim to prescribe to you. 'Their slothful loves and dainty sympathies' is an exquisite line, but you knew *that* when you wrote 'em, and I trifle in pointing such out. Tis altogether the sweetest thing to me you ever wrote—tis all honey—'No wish profaned my overwhelmed heart, Blest hour, it was a Luxury to be.' I recognise feelings, which I may taste again, if tranquility has not taken his flight for ever, and I will not believe but I shall be happy, very happy again. The next poem to your friend is very beautiful —need I instance the pretty fancy of 'the rock's collected tears'—or that original line 'pour'd all its healthful greenness on the soul'—let it be, since you asked me, 'as neighbouring fountains each reflect the whole'—tho' that is somewhat harsh—indeed the ending is not so finish'd as the rest, which if you omit in your forthcoming edition, you will do the volume wrong, and the very binding will cry out. Neither shall you omit the 2 following poems. 'The hour when we shall meet again,' is fine fancy tis true, but fancy catering in the Service of the feeling—fetching from her stores most splendid banquets to satisfy her. Do not, do not omit it. Your sonnet to the *River Otter* excludes those equally beautiful lines, which deserve not to be lost, 'as the tired savage,' &c., and I prefer that copy in your *Watchman*. I plead for its preference.

"Another time I may notice more particularly Lloyd's, Southey's, Dermody's Sonnets. I shrink from them now: my teazing lot makes me too confused for a clear judgment of things, too selfish for sympathy; and these ill-digested, meaningless remarks I have imposed on myself as a task, to lull reflection, as well as to show you I did not neglect reading your valuable present. Return my acknowledgments to Lloyd; you two appear to be about realising an Elysium upon earth, and, no doubt, I shall be happier. Take my best wishes. Remember me most affectionately to Mrs. C., and give little

David Hartley—God bless its little heart!—a kiss for me. Bring him up to know the meaning of his Christian name, and what that name (imposed upon him) will demand of him.

"C. LAMB.

"God love you!

"I write for one thing to say that I shall write no more, till you send me word where you are, for you are so soon to move. My sister is pretty well, thank God. We think of you very often. God bless you, continue to be my correspondent, and I will strive to fancy that this world is *not* 'all barrenness.'"

[Endorsed] Samuel T. Coleridge, Bristol.

The reference to Dr. Anderson, of Isleworth, in a second letter to Coleridge, may form a justification for pointing out that Lamb, in his Essay on *Oxford in the Vacation*, as printed in the *London Magazine* for October,[1] 1820, having made a statement about Dyer and the Doctor, which proved distasteful to a correspondent, Lamb, in the December issue, caused to be inserted under the Lion's Head what follows:—

"Elia requests the Editor to inform W. K. that in his article on Oxford, under the initials G. D., it was his ambition to make more familiar to the public, a character, which, for integrity and single-heartedness, he has long been accustomed to rank among the best patterns of his species.

[1] The passage is suppressed in the collected edition of 1823.

That, if he has failed in the end which he proposed, it was an error of judgment merely. That if, in pursuance of his purpose, he has drawn forth some personal peculiarities of his friend into notice, it was only from conviction that the public, in living subjects especially, do not endure pure panegyric. That the anecdotes, which he produced, were no more than he conceived necessary to awaken attention to character, and were meant solely to illustrate it. That it is an entire mistake to suppose that he undertook the character to set off his own wit or ingenuity. That, he conceives, a candid interpreter might find something intended, beyond a heartless jest. That G. D., however, having thought it necessary to disclaim the anecdote respecting Dr. ——, it becomes him, who never for a moment can doubt the veracity of his friend, to account for it from an imperfect remembrance of some story he heard long ago, and which, happening to tally with his argument, he set down too hastily to the account of G. D. That, from G. D.'s strong affirmations and proofs to the contrary, he is bound to believe it belongs to no part of G. D.'s biography. That the transaction, supposing it true, must have taken place more than forty years ago. That, in consequence, it is not likely to 'meet the eye of many, who might be justly offended.'

"Finally, that what he has said of the Booksellers, referred to a period of many years, in which he has had the happiness of G. D.'s acquaintance; and can have nothing to do with any present or prospective engagements of G. D. with those gentlemen, to the nature of which he professes himself an entire stranger."

II*

"*To Mr. Coleridge.*

"[Southampton Buildings,] August 26th, 1800.

"How do you like this little epigram? It is not my writing, nor had I any finger in it. If you concur with me in thinking it very elegant and very original, I shall be tempted to name the author to you. I will just hint that it is almost or quite a first attempt.

"*Helen repentant too late.*

[Here Miss Lamb's little poem of *Helen* was introduced.]

"Godwin returned from Wicklow the week before last, tho' he did not reach home till the Sunday after. He might much better have spent that time with you.—But you see your invitation would have been too late. He greatly regrets the occasion he mist of visiting you, but he intends to revisit Ireland in the next summer, and then he will certainly take Keswick in his way. I dined with the Heathen on Sunday.

"By-the-by, I have a sort of recollection that somebody, I think *you*, promised me a sight of Wordsworth's Tragedy. I should be very glad of it just now; for I have got Manning with me, and I should like to read it *with him*. But this, I confess, is a refinement. Under any circumstances, alone in Cold Bath Prison, or in the desert island, just when Prospero & his crew had set off, with Caliban in a cage, to Milan, it would be a treat to me to read that play. Manning has read it, so has Lloyd, and all Lloyd's family; but I could not get him to betray his trust by giving *me* a sight of it. Lloyd is sadly deficient in some of those virtuous vices. I have just lit upon a most beautiful fiction of hell punishments by the author of 'Hurtothrumbo,' a mad farce. The inventor imagines that in hell there is a great caldron of hot water, in which a man can scarce hold his finger, and an immense sieve over it, into which the probationary souls are put.

'And all the little souls
Pop through the riddle holes.'

"Mary's love to Mrs. Coleridge—mine to all. N.B.—I pays no postage.

"George Dyer is the only literary character I am happily acquainted with. The oftener I see him, the more deeply I admire him. He is goodness itself. If I could but calculate the precise date of his death, I would write a novel on purpose to make George the hero. I could hit him off to a hair.

"George brought a Dr. Anderson to see me. The Doctor is a very pleasant old man, a great genius for agriculture, one that ties his breeches-knees with Packthread, & boasts of having had disappointments from ministers. The Doctor happened to mention an Epic Poem by one Wilkie, called the 'Epigoniad,' in which he assured us there is not one tolerable line from beginning to end, but all the characters, incidents, &c., verbally copied from *Homer*.[1] George, who had been sitting quite inattentive

[1] "The Epigoniad," by William Wilkie, D.D., 8vo., 1757 and 1769. The same writer produced a volume of "Fables," 8vo., 1758. There is an account of "The Epigoniad" in Burton's "Life of Hume," p. 25.

to the Doctor's criticism, no sooner heard the sound of *Homer* strike his pericraniks, than up he gets, and declares he must see that poem immediately: where was it to be had? An epic poem of 800 [? 8000] lines, and *he* not hear of it! There must be some things good in it, and it was necessary he should see it, for he had touched pretty deeply upon that subject in his criticisms on the Epic. George has touched pretty deeply upon the Lyric, I find; he has also prepared a dissertation on the Drama and the comparison of the English and German theatres. As I rather doubted his competency to do the latter, knowing that his peculiar *turn* lies in the lyric species of composition, I questioned George what English plays he had read. I found that he *had* read Shakspere (whom he calls an original, but irregular, genius), but it was a good while ago; and has dipt into Rowe and Otway, I suppose having found their names in Johnson's Lives at full length; and upon this slender ground he has undertaken the task. He never seem'd even to have heard of Fletcher, Ford, Marlow, Massinger, and the Worthies of Dodsley's Collection; but he is to read all these, to prepare him for bringing out his 'Parallel' in the winter. I find he is also determined to vindicate Poetry from the shackles which Aristotle & some others have imposed upon it, which is very good-natured of him, and very necessary just now! Now I am *touching* so *deeply* upon poetry, can I forget that I have just received from Cottle a magnificent copy of his Guinea Epic.[1] Four-and-twenty Books to read in the

[1] "Alfred," a Poem by Joseph Cottle. A reference occurs to it in a later letter to Coleridge (Oct. 9th, 1800).

dog-days! I got as far as the Mad Monk the first day, & fainted. Mr. Cottle's genius strongly points him to the *Pastoral*, but his inclinations divert him perpetually from his calling. He imitates Southey, as Rowe did Shakspeare, with his 'Good morrow to ye; good master Lieut.' Instead of *a* man, *a* woman, *a* daughter, he constantly writes one a man, one a woman, one his daughter. Instead of *the* king, *the* hero, he constantly writes, he the king, he the hero—two flowers of rhetoric palpably from the 'Joan.' But Mr. Cottle soars a higher pitch: and when he *is* original, it is in a most original way indeed. His terrific scenes are indefatigable. Serpents, asps, spiders, ghosts, dead bodies, staircases made of nothing, with adders' tongues for bannisters—My God! what a brain he must have! He puts as many plums in his pudding as my Grandmother used to do; and then his emerging from Hell's horrors into Light, and treading on pure flats of this earth for twenty-three Books together!

"C. L."

"Mr. Coleridge,
Greta Hall,
Keswick,
Cumberland."

III *

"*To Mr. Southey.*

"Dec. 27, 1798.

"Dear Southey,—Your friend John May[1] has

[1] Southey, in a letter to Cottle, of May, 1797, speaks of him as "a Lisbon acquaintance, and a very valuable one." Perhaps

formerly made kind offers to Lloyd of serving me in the India house by the interest of his friend Sir Francis Baring,—It is not likely that I shall ever put his goodness to the test on my own account, for my prospects are very comfortable. But I know a man, a young man, whom he could serve thro' the same channel, and I think would be disposed to serve if he were acquainted with his case. This poor fellow (whom I know just enough of to vouch for his strict integrity & worth) has lost two or three employments from illness, which he cannot regain; he was once insane, and from the distressful uncertainty of his livelihood, has reason to apprehend a return of that malady—He has been for some time dependant on a woman whose lodger he formerly was, but who can ill afford to maintain him, and I know that on Christmas night last he actually walkd about the streets all night, rather than accept of her Bed which she offer'd him, and offer'd herself to sleep in the kitchen, and that in consequence of that severe cold he is labouring under a bilious disorder, besides a depression of spirits which incapacitates him from exertion when he most needs it—For God's sake, Southey, if it does not go against you to ask favors, do it now, ask it as for me—but do not do a violence to your feelings, because he does not know of this application, and will suffer no disappoint-

---

he assisted Southey in his Brazilian researches; and I take him to have been the same person, at whose house Lamb speaks in one of his letters of Coleridge and himself passing some agreeable winter evenings in London. Coleridge's tailor, whose score Lamb settled, bore the same names.

ment.—What I meant to say was this—there are in the India house what are called *Extra Clerks*, not on the Establishment, like me, but employed in Extra business, by-jobs,—these get about £50 a year, or rather more, but never rise,—a Director can put in at any time a young man in this office, and it is by no means consider'd so great a favor as making an establish'd Clerk. He would think himself as rich as an Emperor if he could get such a certain situation, and be relieved from those disquietudes which I do fear may one day bring back his distemper——

"You know John May better than I do, but I know enough to believe that he is a good man—he did make me that offer that I have mention'd, but you will perceive that such an offer cannot authorize me in applying for another Person.

"But I cannot help writing to you on the subject, for the young man is perpetually before my eyes, and I should feel it a crime not to strain all my petty interest to do him service, tho' I put my own delicacy to the question by so doing—I have made one other unsuccessful attempt already.

"At all events I will thank you to write, for I am tormented with anxiety—

"I suppose you have somehow heard that poor Mary Dollin has poisoned herself, after some interviews with John Reid, the ci-devant Alphonso of her days of hope. How is Edith?

"C. LAMB."

IV*

"*To Mr. Southey.*

[Postmarked] "May 20th 1799.

"Dr. Southey,—Lloyd will now be able to give you an account of himself, so to him I leave you for satisfaction. Great part of his troubles are lightened by the partial recovery of his sister, who had been alarmingly ill with similar diseases to his own. The other part of the family troubles sleeps for the present, but I fear will awake at some future time to *confound* and *disunite*. He will probably tell you all about it. Robert still continues here with me, his father has proposed nothing, but would willingly lure him back with fair professions. But Robert is endowed with a wise fortitude, and in this business has acted quite from himself and wisely acted. His parents must come forward in the end. I like reducing parents to a sense of undutifulness. I like confounding the relations of life. Pray let me see you when you come to town, and contrive to give me some of your company.

"I thank you heartily for your intended presents, but do by no means see the necessity you are under of burthening yourself thereby. You have read old Wither's Supersedeas to small purpose. You object to my pauses being at the end of my lines. I do not know any great difficulty I should find in diversifying or changing my blank verse; but I go upon the model of Shakspere in my Play,[1] and endeavour after a colloquial ease and spirit,

[1] ["John Woodvil," already commenced, but not printed till 1801.]

something like him.[1] I could so easily imitate Milton's versification; but my ear & feeling would reject it, or any approaches to it, in the *drama.* I do not know whether to be glad or sorry that witches have been detected aforetimes in shutting up of wombs. I certainly invented that conceit, and its coincidence with fact is incidental, for I never heard it. I have not seen those verses on Col. Despard—I do not read any newspapers. Are they short, to copy without much trouble? I should like to see them.

"I just send you a few rhymes from my play, the only rhymes in it—a forest-liver giving an account of his amusements:—

'What sports have you in the forest?
Not many,—some few,—as thus,
To see the sun to bed, and see him rise,
Like some hot amourist with glowing eyes,

[1] In the first volume of the "Retrospective Review," p. 15, in the course of a paper on the dramatic criticisms of Rymer, the writer observes:—"The old English feeling of tender beauty has at last begun to revive. Lamb's 'John Woodvil,' despised by the critics, and for a while neglected by the people, awakened those gentle pulses of deep joy, which had long forgotten to beat. Here first, after a long interval, instead of the pompous swelling of inane declamation, the music of humanity was heard in its sweetest tones. The air of freshness breathed over its forest scenes, the delicate grace of its images, its nice disclosure of consolations and venerableness in the nature of man, and the exquisite beauty of its catastrophe, where the strong remorse of the hero is melted into child-like tears, as he kneels on the little hassock where he had often knelt in infancy, is truly Shakespearian." This notice came *from a very friendly pen* in 1820, nineteen years after the first appearance of the volume; and Lamb, who probably saw it, must have been struck by the contrast between the critical tone and that with which the little book was greeted on its original publication, whatever he might privately think of the comparison now flatteringly instituted.

Bursting the lazy bands of sleep that bound him
With all his fires and travelling glories round him:
Sometimes the moon on soft night-clouds to rest,
Like beauty nestling in a young man's breast,
And all the winking stars, her handmaids, keep
Admiring silence, while those lovers sleep:
Sometimes outstretch'd in very idleness,
Nought doing, saying little, thinking less,
To view the leaves, thin dancers upon air,
Go eddying round; and small birds how they fare,
When mother Autumn fills their beaks with corn,
Filch'd from the careless Amalthea's horn;
And how the woods berries and worms provide,
Without their pains, when earth hath nought beside
To answer their small wants;
To view the graceful deer come trooping by,
Then pause, and gaze, then turn they know not why,
Like bashful younkers in society;
To mark the structure of a plant or tree;
And all fair things of earth, how fair they be!' &c. &c.

"I love to anticipate charges of unoriginality: the first line is almost Shakspere's:—

'To have my love to bed & to arise.'
Midsummer Night's Dream.

"I think there is a sweetness in the versification not unlike some rhymes in that exquisite play, and the last line but three is yours:

'An eye
That met the gaze, or turn'd it knew not why.'
Rosamund's Epistle.

"I shall anticipate all my play, and have nothing to shew you.

"An idea for Leviathan.

"Commentators on Job have been puzzled to find out a meaning for Leviathan,—'tis a whale, say some; a crocodile, say others. In my simple conjecture, Leviathan is neither more nor less than the Lord Mayor of London for the time being.

"'Rosamund'[1] sells well in London, maugre the non-reviewal of it.

"I sincerely wish you better health, & better health to Edith. Kind remembrances to her.

"C. LAMB.

"If you come to town by Ash Wensday, you will certainly see Lloyd here—I expect him by that time.

"My sister Mary was never in better health or spirits than now."

"Robert Southey,
Joseph Cottle's,
Bookseller,
High Street,
Bristol."

V*

"*To Mr. Manning.*

"My dear Manning,—The general scope of your letter afforded no indications of insanity, but some particular points raised a scruple. For God's sake don't think any more of 'Independent Tartary.' What are you to do among such Ethiopians? Is there no *lineal descendant* of Prester John?

"Is the chair empty? Is the sword unswayed?—depend upon't they'll never make you their king, as long as any branch of that great stock is remaining. I tremble for your Christianity. They *will* certainly circumcise you. Read Sir John Maundevil's travels to cure you, or come over to England. There is a Tartar-man now exhibiting at Exeter Change. Come

[1] *Rosamund Gray*, printed in 1798.

and talk with him, and hear what he says first. Indeed, he is no very favorable specimen of his Countrymen! But perhaps the best thing you can do, is to *try* to get the idea out of your head. For this purpose repeat to yourself every night, after you have said your prayers, the words Independent Tartary, Independent Tartary, two or three times, and associate with them the *idea of oblivion* ('tis Hartley's method with obstinate memories), or say, Independent, Independent, have I not already got an *Independence?* That was a clever way of the old puritans—pun-divinity. My dear friend, think what a sad pity it would be to bury such *parts* in heathen countries, among nasty, unconversable, horse-belching, Tartar people! Some say, they are Cannibals; and then conceive a Tartar-fellow *eating* my friend, and adding the *cool malignity* of mustard & vinegar! I am afraid 'tis the reading of Chaucer has misled you; his foolish stories about Cambuscan and the ring, and the horse of brass. Believe me, there's no such things, 'tis all the poet's *invention;* but if there were such *darling* things as old Chaucer sings, I would *up* behind you on the Horse of Brass, and frisk off for Prester John's Country. But these are all tales; a Horse of Brass never flew, and a King's daughter never talked with Birds! The Tartars, really, are a cold, insipid, smouchey set. You'll be sadly moped, (if you are not eaten) among them. Pray *try* and cure yourself. Take Hellebore (the counsel is Horace's,[1] 'twas

[1] "Hic ubi cognatorum opibus curisque refectus
Expulit helleboro morbum bilemque meraco"—
Epist. ii. 2, 137.

none of my thought *originally*). Shave yourself oftener. Eat no saffron, for saffron-eaters contract a terrible Tartar-like yellow. Pray, to avoid the fiend. Eat nothing that gives the heart-burn. *Shave the upper lip*. Go about like an European. Read no books of voyages (they're nothing but lies): only now and then a Romance, to keep the fancy *under*. Above all, don't go to any sights of *wild beasts*. *That has been your ruin*. Accustom yourself to write familiar letters on common subjects to your friends in England, such as are of a moderate understanding. And think about common things more. There's your friend Holcroft now, has written a play. You used to be fond of the drama. Nobody went to see it. Notwithstanding this, with an audacity perfectly original, he faces the town down in a preface, that they *did like* it very much. I have heard a waspish punster say, "Sir, why do you not laugh at my jest?" But for a man boldly to face me out with, "Sir, I maintain it, you did laugh at my jest," is a little too much. I have seen H. but once. He spoke of you to me in honorable terms. H. seems to me to be drearily dull. Godwin is dull, but then he has a dash of affectation, which smacks of the coxcomb, and your coxcombs are always agreeable. I supped last night with Rickman, and met a merry *natural* captain, who pleases himself vastly with once having made a Pun at Otaheite in the O. language.[1] 'Tis the same man who said Shak-

[1] Captain, afterward Admiral Burney, who became one of the most constant attendants at Lamb's parties, and whose son, Martin, grew up in his strongest regard, and received the honour of the dedication of the second volume of his works.

speare he liked, because he was so *much of the Gentleman.* Rickman is a man 'absolute in all numbers.' I think I may one day bring you acquainted, if you do not go to Tartary first; for you'll never come back. Have a care, my dear friend, of Anthropophagi! their stomachs are always craving. But if you do go among [them], pray contrive to *think* as soon as you can that you may hang on hand at the Butcher's. 'Tis terrible to be weighed out for 5d. a-pound. To sit at table (the reverse of fishes in Holland), not as a guest, but as a meat.[1]

"God bless you: do come to England. Air and exercise may do great things. Talk with some Minister. Why not your father?

"God dispose all for the best. I have discharged my duty.

"Your sincere fr^{d}.,

"C. LAMB.

19th Feb., 1803, London.

[Endorsed]
Mr. Manning,
Hotel de Paris,
Rue de la Loi,
à Paris.

[1] It seems that Lamb had some vague idea that the Tartars were really anthropophagi, for Alsop says, "Lamb one night wanted to demonstrate, after the manner of Swift, that the Man-t-chou (query, *man-chew?*) Tartars were Cannibals, and that the Chinese were identical with the Celts (Sell Teas.)" But Lamb had no geography; he did not know the map, as he expressed it; and it is quite likely that he had a serious undercurrent of suspicion that, joking apart, human flesh was an article of merchandize and consumption in Tartary. Comp. Shakespear's *Hamlet*, iv., 3.

VI

"*To Mr. Manning.*

"May 10th, 1806.

"My dear Manning,—I didn't know what your going was till I shook a last first with you, & then 'twas just like having shaken hands with a wretch on the fatal scaffold, & when you are down the ladder, you can never stretch out to him again. Mary says you are dead, & there's nothing to do but to leave it to time to do for us in the end what it always does for those who mourn for people in such a case. But she'll see by your letter you are not quite dead. A little kicking and agony, and then——Martin Burney *took me out* a walking that evening, and we talked of Mister Manning; and then I came home and smoked for you, & at twelve o'Clock came home Mary and Monkey Louisa[1] from the play, and there was more talk & more smoking, and they all seemed first-rate characters, because they knew a certain person. But what's the use of talking about 'em? By the time you'll have made your escape from the Kalmuks, you'll have staid so long I shall never be able to bring to your mind who Mary was, who will have died about a year before, nor who the Holcrofts were! me perhaps you will mistake for Phillips, or confound me with Mr. Daw, because you saw us together. Mary (whom you seem to remember yet) is not quite easy that she had not a formal parting from you. I wish it had so happened. But you must bring her a token,

[1] Louisa Martin.

a shawl or something, and remember a sprightly little Mandarin for our mantle piece, as a companion to the Child I am going to purchase at the Museum. She says you saw her writings about the other day, and she wishes you should know what they are. She is doing for Godwin's bookseller[1] twenty of Shakspear's plays, to be made into Children's tales. Six are already done by her, to wit, 'The Tempest,' 'Winter's Tale,' 'Midsummer Night,' 'Much Ado,' 'Two Gentlemen of Verona,' and 'Cymbeline:' & 'The Merchant of Venice' is in forwardness. I have done 'Othello' & 'Macbeth,' and mean to do all the Tragedies. I think it will be popular among the little people. Besides money. It's to bring in 60 guineas. Mary has done them capitally, I think you'd think. These are the humble amusements we propose, while you are gone to plant the cross of Christ among barbarous Pagan anthropophagi. Quam homo homini præstat! but then, perhaps, you'll get murder'd, & we shall die in our beds with a fair literary reputation. Be sure, if you see any of those people, whose heads do grow beneath their shoulders, that you make a draught of them. It will be very curious. O Manning, I am serious to sinking almost, when I think that all those evenings, which you have made so pleasant, are gone perhaps for ever. Four years you talk of, maybe ten, and you may come back & find such alterations! Some circumstance

[1] Godwin had a depôt for books in Hanway Street, whence he subsequently removed to Skinner Street. His wife helped him greatly in the business, and several friends lent their co-operation. Lamb does not seem to have been aware that it was his friend's own speculation.

may grow up to you or to me, that may be a bar to the return of any such intimacy. I dare say all this is Hum, & that all will come back; but indeed we die many deaths before we die, & I am almost sick when I think that such a hold as I had of you is gone. I have friends, but some of 'em are changed. Marriage, or some circumstance, rises up to make them not the same. But I felt sure of you. And that last token you gave me of expressing a wish to have my name joined with yours, you know not how it affected me: like a legacy.

"God bless you in every way you can form a wish. May He give you health, & safety, & the accomplishment of all your objects, and return you again to us, to gladden some fireside or other (I suppose we shall be moved from the Temple). I will nurse the remembrance of your steadiness and quiet, which used to infuse something like itself into our nervous minds. Mary called you our ventilator. Farewell, and take her best wishes & mine.

"One thing more. When you get to Canton, you will most likely see a young friend of mine, Inspector of Teas, named Ball. He is a very good fellow & I should like to have my name talked of in China. Give my kind remembrances to the same Ball.

"Good bye,
"C. L."

"Mr. Manning,
Passenger
On board the Thames
East Indiaman,
Portsmouth."

My reason for reproducing the next is that it has not been given either in the Ainger or my own collection, and appeared in the so-called Fitzgerald edition of 1868 as belonging probably to 1822, or at least finds itself placed thereabout in the order of precedence. Its real season of production was, however, prior to November, 1806, when Coleridge returned home from abroad; for in a letter to Manning of December 5, the same year, Lamb says: "Coleridge is come home, and is going to turn lecturer on Taste at the Royal Institution." The verses, with which the letter winds up, remind us of the *Poetry for Children*, and are poor stuff, regarded as literary products, their interest being limited by their contemporary incidence and atmosphere:—

VII*

Miss Lamb to Miss Wordsworth.

[Temple, late in the Autumn of 1806.]

"My dear Miss Wordsworth,—I thank you, my kind friend, for your most comfortable letter. Till I saw your own handwriting I could not persuade myself that I should do well to write to you, though I have often attempted it; but I always left off dissatisfied with what I had written, and feeling that I was doing an improper thing to intrude upon your sorrow. I wished to tell you that you would one day feel the kind of peaceful state of mind and sweet memory of the dead, which you so happily describe as now almost begun; but I felt that it was improper, and most grating to the feelings of the afflicted, to say to them that the memory of their affection would in time become a constant part, not only of their dream, but of their most wakeful sense of happiness. That you would see every object with and through your lost brother, and that that would at last become a real and everlasting source of comfort to you, I felt, and well knew, from my own experience in sorrow; but till you yourself began to feel this I did not dare tell you so; but I send you some poor lines which I wrote under this conviction of mind, and before I heard Coleridge was returning home. I will transcribe them now, before I finish my letter, lest a false shame prevent me then, for I know they are much worse than they ought to be, written, as they were, with strong feeling, and on such a subject. Every line seems to me to be borrowed; but I had no better way of expressing my thoughts, and I never have the power of altering or amending any thing I have once laid aside with dissatisfaction.

"Why is he wandering on the sea?—
Coleridge should now with Wordsworth be.
By slow degrees he'd steal away
Their woe, and gently bring a ray
(So happily he'd time relief)
Of comfort from their very grief.
He'd tell them that their brother dead,
When years have passèd o'er their head,
Will be remember'd with such holy,
True, and perfect melancholy,
That ever this lost brother John
Will be their hearts' companion."

VIII

To Robert Southey.

"Dear S.,—I have this day deposited with Mr. G. Bedf[d] the essay you suggested to me. I am afraid it is wretchedly inadequate. Who can cram into a strait coop of a review any serious idea of such a vast & magnificent poem as *Excurs[n]*?

"I am myself, too, peculiarly unfit from constitutional causes & want of time. However, it is gone.

"I have 9 or 10 days of my holydays left, but the rains are come.

"Kind remembr[ces] to Mrs. S. & sisters.

"Yours truly,

"C. L."

20th Octob[r], 1814.

[Endorsed]

R. Southey, Esq.,
Keswick,
Near Penrith,
Cumberland.

IX

To Leigh Hunt.

"Dear Sir,—I thank you much for the Curious Volume of Southey, which I return, together with Falstaff's Letters, Elgin Stone Report, & a little work of my own, of which perhaps you have no copy & I have a great many.[1]

"Yours truly,

"C. Lamb."

[In Hunt's hand below.]

Received from C. Lamb, 13th May, 1816.—L. H.

[1] "John Woodvil," &c., 12mo., 1801.

It is probable that many attentive and earnest admirers of *Elia*, if they were to be told that that admirable man and writer was entitled to a place among those who may be considered the modern disciples of Apicius, would ask a little time to consider and refer, before they agreed with such a proposition. In his earlier and poorer days, Lamb, so far as we can make out, had few opportunities of indulging in the pleasures of the table and the palate. But as his means improved, and his circle of friends widened, we easily discover evidences of his appreciation of certain delicacies, which in some cases shewed his taste for such matters to be as idiosyncratic as his views about books. Almost the very latest of his essays was a contribution to the *Athenæum* called "Thoughts on Presents of Game," and as early as 1810 he exhibits an entertaining gusto on the subject of a pig, which had been sent up to him as a present by the Hazlitts from Winterslow. The series of notes to Alsop deals considerably with acknowledgments of oblations of game and "shining" birds; and scattered through the friendly correspondence are numerous hints that Lamb was by no means indifferent to toothsome dishes and flavorous *bonnes bouches*.

The letter now given is a masterpiece of opulent fancy. We have, in the main, an elaborate disquisition on the comparative recommendations of John Dory, Brighton turbot, and cod's head and shoulders, and it is assuredly a masterpiece of its kind. It is an epicurean essay, powerfully illustrating the writer's versatility at what may may be deemed in some respects the finest and most matured period of his literary career. There is nothing finer in *Elia*. The letter is all the more delightfully humorous because it is couched throughout in a perfectly grave tone. The similitude in one place of a cod's head and shoulders from its flakiness to *a sea-onion* is unique. But the whole production deserves study.

X

To Charles Chambers.

[September 1, 1817.][1]

"With regard to a John-dory, which you desire to be particularly informed about, I honour the fish, but it is rather on account of Quin who patronised it, and whose taste (of a *dead* man) I had as lieve go by as anybody's (Apicius and Heliogabalus excepted—this latter started nightingales' tongues and peacocks' brains as a garnish).

"Else in *itself*, and trusting to my own poor single judgment, it hath not that moist mellow oleaginous gliding smooth descent from the

[1] This date is not in Lamb's hand; probably it was supplied by the recipient.

tongue to the palate, thence to the stomach, &c., that your Brighton Turbot hath, which I take to be the most friendly and familiar flavor of any that swims—most genial and at home to the palate.

"Nor has it on the other hand that fine falling off flakiness, that oleaginous peeling off (as it were, like a sea onion), which endears your cod's head & shoulders to some appetites, that manly firmness, combined with a sort of womanish coming-in-pieces, which the same cod's head & shoulders hath, where the whole is easily separable, pliant to a knife or a spoon, but each individual flake presents a pleasing resistance to the opposed tooth—you understand me—these delicate subjects are necessarily obscure.

"But it has a third flavor of its own, perfectly distinct from Cod or Turbot, which it must be owned may to some not injudicious palates render it acceptable—but to my unpractised tooth it presented rather a crude river-fish-flavor, like your Pike or Carp, and perhaps like them should have been tamed & corrected by some laborious & well chosen sauce. Still I always suspect a fish which requires so much of artificial settings-off. Your choicest relishes (like nature's loveliness) need not the foreign aid of ornament, but are when unadorned (that is, with nothing but a little plain anchovy & a squeeze of lemon) are then adorned the most. However, I shall go to Brighton again next Summer, and shall have an opportunity of correcting my judgment, if it is not sufficiently informed. I can only say that when Nature was pleased to make the John Dory so notoriously deficient in outward graces (as to be sure he is the very Rhinoceros of fishes, the ugliest dog that swims, except perhaps the Sea Satyr, which I never saw, but which they say is terrible), when she formed him with so few external advantages, she might have bestowed a more elaborate finish in his parts internal, & have given him a relish, a sapor, to recommend him, as she made Pope a Poet to make up for making him crooked.

"I am sorry to find that you have got a knack of saying things which are not true to shew your wit. If I had no wit but what I must shew at the expence of my virtue or my modesty, I had as lieve be as stupid as . . . at[1] the Tea Warehouse. Depend upon it, my dear Chambers, that an ounce of integrity at our death-bed will stand us in more avail than all the wit of Congreve or . . . For instance, you tell me a fine story about Truss, and his playing at Leamington, which I know to be false, because I have advice from Derby that he was whipt through the Town on that very day you say he appeared in some character or other, for robbing an old woman at church of a seal ring. And Dr. Parr has been two months dead. So it won't do to scatter these untrue stories about among people that know any thing. Besides, your forte is not invention. It is *judgment*, particularly shown in your choice of dishes. We seem in that instance born under one star. I like you for liking hare. I esteem you for disrelishing minced veal. Liking is too cold a word. I love you for your noble attachment to the fat unctuous juices of deer's flesh & the green unspeakable of turtle. I honour you for your endeavours to esteem and approve

[1] So in the original. Query Bye, one of Lamb's colleagues.

of my favorite, which I ventured to recommend to you as a substitute for hare, bullock's heart, and I am not offended that you cannot taste it with *my* palate. A true son of Epicurus should reserve one taste peculiar to himself. For a long time I kept the secret about the exceeding deliciousness of the marrow of boiled knuckle of veal, till my tongue weakly ran riot in its praises, and now it is prostitute & common.—But I have made one discovery which I will not impart till my dying scene is over, perhaps it will be my last mouthful in this world, delicious thought, enough to sweeten (or rather make savoury) the hour of death. It is a little square bit about this size in or near the knuckle bone of a fried joint of . . . fat I can't call it nor lean neither altogether, it is that beautiful compound, which Nature must have made in Paradise Park venison, before she separated the two substances, the dry & the oleaginous, to punish sinful mankind; Adam ate them entire & inseparate, and this little taste of Eden in the knuckle bone of a fried . . . seems the only relique of a Paradisaical state. When I die, an exact description of its topography shall be left in a cupboard with a key, inscribed on which these words, 'C. Lamb dying imparts this to C. Chambers as the only worthy depository of such a secret.' You'll drop a tear. . . ."

[Endorsed]
Mr. C. Chambers,
Leamington,
near Warwick.

Our next is a note to the publishers of Lamb's Works, as they were called on the title-page, in 1818, in two duodecimo volumes. The book was nearly out of the printer's hands.

XI *

C. Lamb to the Messrs. Ollier.

[28th May, 1818.]

"Dear Sir,—The last sheet is finish'd. All that remains is the Title page and the Contents, which should be uniform with vol. 1. Will you be kind enough to see to it? There is a Sonnet to come in by way of dedication. I have not the sheet, so I cannot make out the Table of Contents, but it may be done from the various Essays, Letters, &c. by you, or the Printer, as thus. [Here follows a rough sketch of the writer's plan.]

"Yours in Haste. "C. LAMB.

"Let me see the last proof, sonnet, &c."

Messrs. Ollier, Booksellers,
Vere Street, Oxford Street.

The letter was directed in the singular number, that either of the brothers might open it. The Olliers figure in the correspondence during some years.

A note of about the same date from Miss Lamb to Mrs. J. D. Collier, mother of the antiquary, was written on behalf of the only unmarried Miss Fricker.

XII

Miss Lamb to Mrs. Collier.

[No date.]

"Dear Mrs. C.,—This note will be given you by a young friend[1] of mine, whom I wish you would employ; she has commenced business as a mantua-maker and if you and my girls[2] would try her, I think she would fit you all three, and it will be doing her an essential service. She is, I think, very deserving, and if you procure work for her, among your friends and acquaintances, so much the better. My best love to you and my girls. We are both well.

"Yours affectionately,

"MARY LAMB."[3]

Miss Betham, or, indeed, more than one of the six-and-thirty feet of daughters, Miss Mary Hazlitt, younger daughter of the painter, and Mrs., afterward Lady, Stoddart, conspired, during many years, to vex the soul of Lamb by their perpetual calls upon him to act the part of a literary censor; and certain of Mrs. Stoddart's performances in the shape of novels, and Miss Hazlitt's only one, even with this

[1] Sister of the three "milliners of Bath," Mrs Coleridge, Mrs. Southey, and Mrs. Lovell.

[2] Mrs. Collier's daughters.

[3] See Collier's Diary, p 80. The writer notes his recollection that Miss Fricker remained seven years in his family, and then returned to Bristol Compare Cottle's Recollections of S. T. Coleridge, 1837, p. 2.

succour and an inclusive word of recommendation to some publisher, never reached the printer's hands. They belonged to a short-lived type, and became no better than dead leaves. In turning over the pages of two or three unpublished romances by Mrs. Stoddart, one is struck by the wholesale castigation of the text in Lamb's hand and by the marginal expressions of impatience which he has left behind him—the sole features of interest for us in these feeble literary efforts of an amiable lady of the old school.

Is it more than justice, however, to recollect that the Lambs were by tradition and training of this set. Much of their early work, the *Poetry for Children* and *Mrs. Leicester's School*, and even of Lamb's somewhat later efforts, his *Prince Dorus* and *Beauty and the Beast*, partook of the same colourless insipidity; and had it not been for that marvellously fruitful communion with other minds, and the *Elia* and the *Letters*, the name would certainly not hold the rank which it does at the present moment.

The "Little Barbara," afterward Mrs. Edwards, to whom the following letter was addressed, was the youngest sister of Matilda, one of the regular correspondents of Lamb himself.

XIII *

THE BETHAM CORRESPONDENCE.

"*Miss Lamb to Miss Barbara Betham.*[1]

"Novr. 2, 1814.

"It is very long since I have met with such an agreeable surprise as the sight of your letter, my kind young friend, afforded me. Such a nice letter as it is too. And what a pretty hand you write. I congratulate you on this attainment with great pleasure, because I have so often felt the disadvantage of my own wretched handwriting.

"You wish for London news. I rely upon your sister Ann for gratifying you in this respect, yet I have been endeavouring to recollect whom you might have seen here, and what may have happened to them since, and this effort has only brought the image of little Barbara Betham, unconnected with any other person, so strongly before my eyes that I seem as if I had no other subject to write upon. Now I think I see you with your feet propped upon the fender, your two hands spread out upon your knees—an attitude you always chose when we were in familiar confidential conversation together—telling me long stories of your own home, where now you say you are 'Moping on with the same thing every day,' and which then presented nothing but pleasant recollections to your mind. How well I remember your quiet steady face bent over your book. One day, conscience struck at having wasted so much of your pre-

[1] From the autograph.

cious time in reading, and feeling yourself, as you prettily said, 'quite useless to me,' you went to my drawers and hunted out some unhemmed pocket-hankerchiefs, and by no means could I prevail upon you to resume your story books till you had hemmed them all. I remember, too, your teaching my little maid to read—your sitting with her a whole evening to console her for the death of her sister; and that she in her turn endeavoured to become a comforter to you, the next evening, when you wept at the sight of Mrs. Holcroft, from whose school you had recently eloped because you were not partial to sitting in the stocks. Those tears, and a few you once dropped when my brother teased you about your supposed fondness for an apple dumpling, were the only interruptions to the calm contentedness of your unclouded brow. We still remain the same as you left us, neither taller nor wiser, or perceptibly older, but three years must have made a great alteration in you. How very much, dear Barbara, I should like to see you!

"We still live in Temple Lane, but I am now sitting in a room you never saw. Soon after you left us we we[re] distressed by the cries of a cat, which seemed to proceed from the garrets adjoining to ours, and only separated from ours by a locked door on the farther side of my brother's bedroom, which you know was the little room at the top of the kitchen stairs. We had the lock forced and let poor puss out from behind a pannel of the wainscot, and she lived with us from that time, for we were in gratitude bound to keep her, as she had introduced us to four untenanted, unowned rooms, and by degrees we have taken possession of these unclaimed apartments—First putting up lines to dry our clothes, then moving my brother's bed into one of these, more commodious than his own room. And last winter, my brother being unable to pursue a work he had begun, owing to the kind interruptions of friends who were more at leisure than himself, I persuaded him that he might write at his ease in one of these rooms, as he could not then hear the door knock, or hear himself denied to be at home, which was sure to make him call out and convict the poor maid in a fib. Here, I said, he might be almost really not at home. So I put in an old grate, & made him a fire in the largest of these garrets, and carried in one table, and one chair, and bid him write away, and consider himself as much alone as if he were in a new lodging in the midst of Salisbury Plain, or any other wide unfrequented place where he could expect few visitors to break in upon his solitude. I left him quite delighted with his new acquisition, but in a few hours he came down again with a sadly dismal face. He could do nothing, he said, with those bare whitewashed walls before his eyes. He could not write in that dull unfurnished prison.

"The next day, before he came home from his office, I had gathered up various bits of old carpetting to cover the floor; and, to a little break the blank look of the bare walls, I hung up a few old prints that used to ornament the kitchen, and after dinner, with great boast of what an improvement I had made, I took

Charles once more into his new study. A week of busy labours followed, in which I think you would not have disliked to have been our assistant. My brother & I almost covered the walls with prints, for which purpose he cut out every print from every book in his old library, coming in every now and then to ask my leave to strip a fresh poor author—which he might not do, you know, without my permission, as I am elder sister. There was such pasting, such consultation where their portraits, and where the series of pictures from Ovid, Milton, & Shakespear would show to most advantage, and in what obscure corner authors of humbler note might be allowed to tell their stories. All the books gave up their stores but one, a translation from Ariosto, a delicious set of four & twenty prints, & for which I had marked out a conspicuous place; when lo! we found at the moment the scissars were going to work that a part of the poem was printed at the back of every picture. What a cruel disappointment! To conclude this long story about nothing, the poor despised garret is now called the print room, and is become our most favorite sitting room.

"Your sister Ann will tell you that your friend Louisa is going to France. Miss Skepper is out of town, Mrs. Reynolds desires to be remembered to you, and so does my neighbour Mrs. Norris, who was your doctress when you were unwell, her three little children are grown three big children. The Lions still live in Exeter Change. Returning home through the Strand, I often hear them roar about twelve oclock at night. I never hear them without thinking of you, because you seemed so pleased with the sight of them, & said your young companions would stare when you told them you had seen a Lion.

"And now my dear Barbara fare well, I have not written such a long letter a long time, but I am very sorry I had nothing amusing to write about. Wishing you may pass happily through the rest of your school days, and every future day of your life,

"I remain, your affectionate Friend,

"M. LAMB.

"My brother sends his love to you, with the kind remembrance your letter shewed you have of us as I was. He joins with me in respects to your good father & mother, and to your brother John, who, if I do not mistake his name, is your tall young brother who was in search of a fair lady with a large fortune. Ask him if he has found her yet. You say you are not so tall as Louisa—you must be, you cannor so degenerate from the rest of your family. Now you have begun, I shall hope to have the pleasure of hearing from [you] again. I shall always receive a letter from you with very great delight."

XIV*

C. Lamb to Miss Matilda Betham.

"Dear Miss Betham,—I have sent your *very pretty lines* to Southey in a frank, as you requested. Poor S., what a grievous loss he must have had! Mary and I rejoyce in the prospect of seeing you soon in Town. Let us be among the very first persons you come to see. Believe me that you can have no friends who respect & love you more than ourselves. Pray present our kind remembrances to Barbara and to all to whom you may think they will be acceptable.

"Yours very sincerely,

"C. Lamb.

"Have you seen *Christabel* since its publication?"

E. I. H., 1st June, 1816.

The subjoined, from Miss Lamb, was written subsequently to the removal of the brother and sister from the Temple and the alteration of their reception-day.

XV*

Miss Lamb to the Same.

[20, Russell Street, Covent Garden, about 1818.]

"My dear Matilda,—Coleridge has given me a very chearful promise that he will wait on Lady Jerningham any day you will be pleased to appoint; he offered to write to you; but I found it was to be done *tomorrow*, and as I am pretty well acquainted with his tomorrows, I thought good to let you know his determination *today*. He is in town today, but as he is often going to Hammersmith for a night or two, you had better perhaps send the invitation through me, and I will manage it for you as well as I can. You had better let him have four or five days' previous notice, and you had better send the invitation as soon as you can; for he seems tolerably well just now. I mention all these betters, because I wish to do the best I can for you, perceiving, as I do, it is a thing you have set your heart upon. He dined one [d]ay in company with Catilana ([1] is that the way you spell her Italian name?—I am reading Sallust, and had like to have written Catiline). How I should have liked, and how you would have liked, to have seen Coleridge and Catilana together!

"You have been very good of late to let me come and see you so seldom, and you are a little goodish to come so seldom here, because you stay away from a kind motive. But if you stay away always, as I fear you mean to do, I would not give one pin for your good intentions. In plain words, come and see me very soon; for though I be not sensitive as some people, I begin to feel strange qualms for having driven you from me.

"Yours affectionately,

"M. Lamb.

"*Wednesday.*

"Alas! Wednesday shines no more to me now.

"Miss Duncan played famously in the new comedy, which went off as famously. By the way, she put in a spiteful piece of wit, I verily believe of her own head; and methought she stared me full in the face. The words were 'As silent as an author in company.' Her hair and herself looked remarkably well."

[Endorsed]

Miss Betham,

49 Upper Marybone Street.

[1] Catalani, who married M. Valabrègue.

The Miss Duncan named in the postscript was the actress who took part, in the absence of Mrs. Jordan, in Holcroft's play of the *Vindictive Man*, which was brought out and damned in 1806.

The next letter is not only now exhibited for the first time as it came from Lamb's pen; but the earliest opportunity is taken to correct the misapprehension, into which all the editors have been betrayed, of confounding it with that of June 1st, 1816.

XVI *

C. Lamb to the Same.

[Postmark illegible. ? East India House, no date, about 1824.]

"Mary goes to her Place on Sunday—I mean your maid, foolish Mary; she wants a very little brain only to be an excellent serv$^{t.}$ She is excellently calculated for the country, where no body has brains.

"Dear Miss Betham,—All this while I have been tormenting myself with the thought of having been ungracious to you, and you have been all the while accusing yourself. Let us absolve one another, & be quits. My head is in such a state from incapacity for business that I certainly know it to be my duty not to undertake the veriest trifle in addition. I hardly know how I can go on. I have tried to get some redress by explaining my health, but with no great success. No one can tell how ill I am because it does not come out to the exterior of my face, but lies in my skull, deep & invisible. I wish I was leprous & black-jaundiced skin-over, and that all was as well within as my cursed looks. You must not think me worse than I am. I am determined not to be overset, but to give up business rather, and get 'em to give me a trifle for services past. O, that I had been a shoemaker, or a baker, or a man of large independent fortune. O darling laziness! heaven of Epicurus! Saints' Everlasting Rest! that I could drink vast potations of thee thro' unmeasured Eternity. Otium vel *cum* vel *sine* dignitate. Scandalous, dishonorable—any kind of *repose*. I stand not upon the *dignified sort*. Accursed, damned desks, trade, commerce, business! Inventions of the old original busy-body, brain-working Satan—Sabbathless, restless Satan!

"A curse relieves—do you ever try it?

"A strange letter this to write to a lady; but mere honeyed sentences will not distil. I dare not ask who revises in my stead. I have drawn you into a scrape and am ashamed; but I know no remedy. My unwellness must be my apology. God bless you (tho' He curse the India House and fire it to the *ground*) and may no unkind Error creep into 'Marie'! May all its readers like it as well as I do, and every body about you like its kind author no worse. Why the devil am I never to have a chance of scribbling my own free thoughts, verse or prose, again? Why must I write of Tea & Drugs, & Piece goods & bales of Indigo? Farewell.

"C. LAMB."

The following letter to the same lady is also safely assignable, I conceive, to that period just antecedent to Lamb's retirement from the India House, when he began to grow restless and impatient, and to give vent to his feelings in no measured terms. Of course it is more or less hazardous to fix the date within this certain space, since even so early as the end of 1818, in writing to Coleridge, Lamb inveighs against official drudgery and confinement.

XVII

The Same to the Same.

"Dr Miss B.,—Mr. Hunter has this morning put into a Parcel *all I have received from you* at various times, including a sheet of notes from the Printer and two fair sheets of *Mary*. I hope you will receive them safe. The poem I will continue to look over, but must request you to provide for the rest. I cannot attend to anything but the most simple things. I am very much unhinged indeed. Tell K. I saw Mrs. K. yesterday and she was well. You must write to Hunter if you are in a hurry for the notes, &c.

"Yours sincerely, "C. L.

"*Saturday*.

"Shall I direct the Printer to send you fair sheets, as they are printed?"

A second letter to the same lady, without note of time, but written while Lamb was still allowing himself to be retained as Miss Betham's literary counsel, has not yet found its way into any of the editions.

XVIII

Miss Lamb to Miss Matilda Betham.

"My dear Miss Betham,—My brother and myself return you a thousand thanks for your kind communication. We have read your poem many times over with increased interest, and very much wish to see you to tell you how highly we have been pleased with it. May we beg one favour? I keep the manuscript in the hope that you will grant it. It is that, either now or when the whole poem is completed, you will read it over with us. When I say with *us*, of course I mean Charles. I know that you have many judicious friends, but I have so often known my brother spy out errors in a manuscript which has passed through many judicious hands, that I shall not be easy if you do not permit him to look yours carefully through with you; and also you *must* allow him to correct the press for you.

"If I knew where to find you I would call upon you. Should you feel nervous at the idea of meeting Charles in the capacity of a *severe censor*, give me a line, and I will come to you anywhere and convince you in five minutes that he is even timid, stammers, and can scarcely speak for modesty and fear of giving pain when he finds himself placed in that kind of office. Shall I appoint a time to see you here when he is from home? I will send him out any time you will name; indeed, I am always naturally alone till four o'clock. If you are nervous about coming, remember I am equally so about the liberty I have taken, and shall be till we meet and [throw] off our mutual fears.

"Yours most affectionately,

"M. LAMB."

The next letter to the same lady, within my present knowledge, is of August 23, 1833. It has never hitherto appeared in its integrity or in its true order. It is one of the Edmonton series, and was posterior to Emma Isola's marriage.

XIX

C. Lamb to the Same.

"Dear Miss B.,—Your Bridal verses are very beautiful. Emma shall have them, as here corrected, when they return. They are in France. The verses, I repeat, are sweetly pretty. I know nobody in these parts that wants a servant; indeed, I have no acquaintance in this new place, and rarely come to town. The rule of Christ's Hospital is rigorous, that the marriage certificate of the parents be produced, previous to the presentation of a boy, so that your renowned Protegè has no chance. Never trouble yourself about Dyer's neighbour. He will only tell you a parcel of fibs, and is impracticable to any advice. He has been long married and parted, and has to pay his wife a weekly allowance to this day, besides other incumbrances.

"In haste and headake,

"Yours, [Signature lost.]

"Aug[t] 23, 1833."

XX

The Same to the Same.

[January 29, 1834.]

"Dear Miss M.,—I have had a letter from your sister Mary, and come to town on Monday next in consequence. I shall take an early chop in town, and will call upon you about 2 or 3 in the afternoon. My poor Mary is terribly ill again.

"Yours,

"C. LAMB."

[Endorsed]
Miss Betham,
Vicarage,
near the Church,
Islington.

THE NORRIS CORRESPONDENCE.

XXI

C. Lamb to Mrs. Norris.

"Dear Mrs. N.,—Mary will be in town this Even[g] or to-morrow morn[g]. As she wants to see you about another business. She will in the meantime enquire respecting the young woman.

"Yours sincerely,

E. I. H. "C. LAMB."
26 Mar. 1822.
Mrs. Norris,
Tanfield Court, Temple.

The next in order of date was seemingly despatched by Lamb soon after their return from France in 1825, when he was still labouring under the humorous idiosyncrasy of interlarding his sentences with very bad French, or rather an Anglo-French doggrel of his own. Our text follows the original among the Norris papers:—

XXII

The Same to Miss Norris.

[No superscription.] [1825.]

" Hypochondriac. We can't reckon avec any ertainty for une heure . . . as follows:

England.[1]

" I like the Taxes when they're not oo many,
I like a sea-coal fire when not too dear;
I like a beefsteak, too, as well as any,
Have no objection to a pot of beer;
I like the *weather when it s not too rainy*,
That is, I like two months of every year.

Italy.

" I also like to dine on becaficas,
To see the sun set, sure he'll rise to-morrow,
Not through a misty morning twinkling weak as
A drunken man's dead eye in maudlin sorrow.
But with all heaven t'himself; that day will break as
Beauteous as cloudless, nor be forced to borrow
That sort of farthing candlelight which glimmers
Where reeking London's smoky cauldron simmers.

" Kind regards to Mama & remembrances to Frere Richard. Dieu remercie mon frere can't

[1] From Byron's *Beppo*, slightly out of order.

lizer Fransay. I have written this letter with a most villainous pen—called a Patent one.

"En finis je remarque I was not offensé a votre fransay et I was not embarrassé to make it out. Adieu.

"I have not quite done that——instead of your company in Miss Norris; epistle has determined me to come if heaven, earth, & myself can compass it. Amen."

[No signature.]

XXIII

Mary Lamb to Mrs. Norris.

The succeeding letter from Miss Lamb furnishes a curious account and picture of the brother's and sister's experiences in one of their seaside holiday excursions, posterior to that of 1823, when we know that they also went to Hastings. It is in the writer's usual manner—frank, gossiping, and affectionate:—

"Hastings, at Mrs. Gibbs, York Cottage, Priory, No. 4. [1825 6.]

"My dear Friend,—Day after day has passed away, and my brother has said 'I will write to Mrs. Norris to-morrow,' and therefore I am resolved to write to *Mrs. Norris* to-day, and trust him no longer. We took our places for Sevenoaks, intending to remain here all night in order to see Knole, but when we got there we chang'd our minds, and went on to Tunbridge Wells. About a mile short of the Wells the coach stopped at a little inn, and I saw lodgings to let on a little, very little house opposite. I ran over the way, and secured them before the coach drove away, and we took immediate possession: it proved a very comfortable place, and we remained there nine days. The first evening, as we were wandering about, we met a lady, the wife of one of the India House clerks, with whom we had been slightly acquainted some years ago, which slight acquaintance has been ripened into a great intimacy during the nine pleasant days that we passed at the Wells. She and her two daughters went with us in an open chaise to Knole, and as the chaise held only five, we mounted Miss James upon a little horse, which she rode famously. I was very much pleased with Knole, and still more with Penshurst, which we also visited. We saw Frant and the Rocks, and made much use of your Guide Book, only Charles lost his way once going by the map. We were in constant exercise the whole time, and spent our time so pleasantly that when we came here on Monday we missed our new friends and found ourselves very dull. We are by the seaside in a *still less* house, and we have exchanged a very pretty landlady for a very ugly one, but she is equally attractive to us. We eat turbot, and we drink smuggled Hollands, and we walk up hill and down hill all day long. In the little intervals of rest that we allow ourselves I teach Miss James french; she picked up a few words during her foreign Tour with us, and she has had a hankering after it ever since.

"We came from Tunbridge Wells in a Post-chaise, and would have seen Battle Abbey on the way, but it is only shewn on a Monday. We are trying to coax Charles into a Monday's excursion.

And Bexhill we are also thinking about. Yesterday evening we found out by chance the most beautiful view I ever saw. It is called 'The Lovers' Seat.' . . . You have been here, therefore you must have seen [it, or] is it only Mr. and Mrs. Faint who have visited Hastings? [Tell Mrs.] Faint that though in my haste to get housed I d[ecided on] . . . ice's lodgings, yet it comforted all th . . . to know that I had a place in view.

"I suppose you are so busy that it is not fair to ask you to write me a line to say how you are going on. Yet if any one of you have half an hour to spare for that purpose, it will be most thankfully received. Charles joins with me in love to you all together, and to each one in particular upstairs and downstairs.

"Yours most affectionately,

"M. Lamb.

"June 18."

[Endorsed]

Randal Norris, Esq.,
Inner Temple, London.
For Mrs. N.

There is an interval of a full decade between the last letter and those which follow, and which illustrate more or less valuably the latest years as well of Charles as of his sister.

It is possible that some intervening matter has disappeared, but let us bear in mind that Lamb—nay, both, were rather spasmodic in their communications all round, especially toward the last.

Here is a note to Mrs. Norris, enclosing one which had come from Joseph Jekyll, acknowledging the receipt of a gift of the second series of *Elia*. Autograph-collectors will mark what is said of their pursuit! Emma is of course Miss Isola, afterward Mrs. Moxon.

XXIV

C. Lamb to Mrs. Norris.

"Dear Mrs. Norris,—I wrote to Jekyll, and sent him an *Elia*. This is his kind answer. So you see that he will be glad to see *any of you* that shall be in town, and will arrange, if you prefer it, to accompany you. If you are at Brighton, Betsey will forward this. I have cut off the name at the bottom to give to a foolish autograph fancier. Love to you all. Emma sends her very kindest.

"C. LAMB."

[Postmarked] July 10, 1833.

[*Enclosure.*]

"My Dear Sir,—I must not lose A moment in thanking you for another volume of your delightful pen, which reached me this Morning, but I hope not the last Essays of Elia.

"For Faint I had much Regard, and it delights me to hear he has manifested such good Feelings towards Mrs. Norris and her Daughters. On their Visit to London, it would afford me much pleasure to see them, and, still more, if you could contrive to accompany them.

"Poor George Dyer, blind, but as usual chearful and content, often gives, on my Enquiry, good accounts of you. With my Regards to Mrs. Norris,

[Signature cut off.]

"Spring Garden,
"Thursday, June 27, 1833.
"C. Lamb, Esq."

The excessive rarity of letters addressed *to* the Lambs is probably well known; and the present only escaped by being forwarded to a friend.

XXV

When the next subscribed *Elia* was written, Lamb had paid a visit to Mrs. and Miss Norris at Widford, near Ware, and it is manifest that they, or one of them, had expressed, perhaps for the first time in all these years, a desire to see some of his literary productions:—

The Same to the Same.

"Mrs. Walden's, Church Street, Edmonton.
[July 18, 1833.]

"Dear Mrs. Norris,—I got home safe. Pray accept these little books, and some of you *give me a line to say you received them.* Love to all, and thanks for three agreeable days. I send them this afternoon (Tuesday) by Canter's coach. Are the little girls packed safe? They can come in straw, and have eggs under them. Ask them to lie soft, 'cause eggs smash.

"Elia."

"The first volume printed here 'Poetry for Children'] is not to be had for love or money, not even an American edition of it, and the second volume, American also, to suit with it. It is much the same as the London one."

XXVI

We are not at liberty to question that Lamb was again at Widford in the last year of his life, and that he there drew up, for the information of his entertainers, a bibliography of his works as follows:

"*Blank Verse* (with C. Lloyd).
"*Rosamund Gray*, a tale.
"*John Woodvil*, a tragedy.
"Those 3 printed separately, together with Poems and Essays, & *Mr. H.*, a farce, were collected in two volumes call'd *Works of C. Lamb.*
"*Album Verses.*
"*Elia's Essays.*
"*Last Essays of Elia.*
"*Adventures of Ulysses.*
"*Poetry* (with Mary L.).
"*Tales of Shaksp.* (Do.).
"*Mrs. Leicester's School* (Do.).
} all for Children.
besides *The Pawnbroker's Daughter*, a farce, and numberless nonsense, prose and *worse*, scatter'd about in Magazines and Newspapers, never got together, irrepa[ra]bly gone to oblivion.

"These are all the follies I can remember just now.

"C. LAMB.

"Widford, 3 Nov., 1834."

XXVII

On his return from this second visit he made up a package of all such of his own books as he could find at home, and sent them off to Widford.

The Same to the Same.

[Edmonton: November, 1834.]

"Dear Mrs. Norris,—I found Mary on my return not worse, and she is now no better. I send all my nonsense I could scrape together, and wish your young ladies well thro' them. I hope they will like 'Amwell.' Be in no hurry to return them. Six months hence will do. Remember me kindly to them and to Richard. Also to Mary and her cousin.

"Yours truly,

"C. LAMB.

"Pray give me a line to say you receiv'd 'em. I send 'em Wednesday 19th, from the Roebuck."

About six *weeks* subsequently to this note Lamb died (December 26, 1834), and we have now to do with three letters which derive their principal importance from being, as I apprehend, the only remaining documents illustrating the last days of Charles's sister and life-companion. When the third was written by Miss James, the old and faithful attendant recommended by the Kenneys, Miss Lamb was no longer capable, it may be more than inferred, of using her pen, and was not in a state of mind to bear much conversation or any excitement.

XXVIII

Mary Lamb to Miss Norris.

[41 Alpha Road, Regent's Park] Christmas Day [1841].

"My dear Jane,—Many thanks for your kind presents—your Michalmas goose. I thought Mr. Moxon had written to thank you—the turkeys and nice apples came yesterday.

"Give my love to your dear Mother. I was unhappy to find your note in the basket, for I am always thinking of you all, and wondering when I shall ever see any of you again.

"I long to shew you what a nice snug place I have got into—in the midst of a pleasant little garden. I have a room for myself and my old books on the ground floor, and a little bed-room up two pairs of stairs. When you come to town, if you have not time to go [to] the Moxons, an Omnibus from the Bell and Crown in Holborn would [bring] you to our door in [a] quarter of an hour. If your dear Mother does not venture so far, I will contrive to pop down to see [her]. Love and all seasonable wishes to your sister and Mary, &c. I am in the midst of many friends—Mr. & Mrs. Kenney, Mr. & Mrs. Hood, Bar[r]on Field & his brother Frank, & their wives &c., all within a short walk.

"If the lodger is gone, I shall have a bedroom

will hold two! Heaven bless & preserve you all in health and happiness many a long year.

"Yours affectionately,

"M. A. LAMB."

[Endorsed]
Miss Jane Norris,
Widford, near Ware,
Hertfordshire.

XXIX

The Same to the Same.

"Oct. 3, 1842.

"My dear Jane Norris,—Thanks, many thanks, my dear friend, for your kind remembrances. What a nice Goose! That, and all its accompaniments in the basket, we all devoured; the two legs fell to my share!!!

"Your chearful [letter,] my Jane, made me feel 'almost as good as new.'

"Your Mother and I *must meet again*. Do not be surprized if I pop in again for a half-hour's call some fine frosty morning.

"Thank you, dear Jane, for the happy tidings that my *old* friend Miss Bangham is alive, an[d] that Mary is still with you, unmarried. Heaven bless you all.

"Love to Mother, *Betsey*, Mary, &c. How I do long to see you.

"I am always your affec[ately] grateful friend,

"MARY ANN LAMB.

"No. 41. A[l]pha Road."

[Endorsed in another hand]:
Miss Jane Norris,
Goddard House, Widford,
near Haddum [Hadham], Herts.

XXX

Miss James to Miss Norris.

"41 Alpha Road, Regent's Park,
London, July 25, 1843.

"Madam,—Miss Lamb having seen the Death of your dear Mother in the times News Paper is most anxious to hear from or to see one of you, as she wishes to know how you intend settling yourselves, and to have a full account of your dear Mother's last illness. She was much shocked on reading of her death, and appeared very vexed that she had not been to see her, [and] wanted very much to come down and see you both; but we were really afraid to let her take the journey. If either of you are coming up to town, she would be glad if you would call upon her, but should you not be likely to come soon, she would be very much pleased, if one of you would have the goodness to write a few lines to her, as she is most anxious about you. She begs you to excuse her writing to you herself, as she don't feel equal to it; she asked me yesterday to write for her. I am happy to say she is at present pretty well, although your dear Mother's death appears to dwell much upon her mind. She desires her kindest love to you both, and hopes to hear from you very soon, if you are equal to writing. I sincerely hope you will oblige her, and am,

"Madam,

"Your obedient, &c.,

"SARAH JAMES.

"Pray don't invite her to come down to see you."

[Endorsed on envelope]

Miss Norris,
Goddard House, Widford,
near Ware, Hertfordshire.

XXXI

The correspondence of the Lambs with the Kenney family was rather suspected, than absolutely ascertained, till of late years. Two letters to Kenney were furnished by the present writer, and Canon Ainger has added a third, a remarkably beautiful one,—a bipartite production to Mrs. Kenney and her daughter, Sophy Holcroft, afterward married to Dr. Jefferson of Leamington. I have met this lady more than once. Now I cap this triplet with a fourth and fifth, the former from Miss Lamb to Mrs. Kenney, also composed, of course, after the visit to France in 1822, and the return of Miss Lamb herself in September. The second division of the letter, directed to Sophy Holcroft, recalls those delightful effusions of Southey to his children. I regret my inability to decipher the whole of Miss Fanny Kelly's accompaniment.

Miss Lamb to Mrs. Kenney.[1]

[About October, 1822.]

"My dear Friend,—How do you like Harwood?[2] Is he not a noble boy? I congratulate

[1] From the original autograph. The letter from Miss Lamb is accompanied by one from her brother to Kenney, and by a few lines from Miss Fanny Kelly, the celebrated actress. Lamb's letter was printed in Hazlitt's edition of the Correspondence for the first time.

[2] Harwood Holcroft.

you most heartily on this happy meeting, and only wish I were present to witness it. Come back with Harwood, I am dying to see you—we will talk, that is, you shall talk and I will listen from ten in the morning till twelve at night. My thoughts are often with you, and your children's dear faces are perpetually before me. Give them all one additional kiss every morning for me. Remember there's one for Louisa, one to Ellen, one to Betsy,[1] one to Sophia, one to James, one to Teresa, one to Virginia, and one to Charles. Bless them all! When shall I ever see them again? Thank you a thousand times for all your kindness to me. I know you will make light of the trouble my illness gave you; but the recollection of it often sits heavy on my heart. If I could ensure my health, how happy should I be to spend a month with you every summer!

"When I met Mr. Kenn[e]y there, I sadly repented that I had not dragged you on to Dieppe with me. What a pleasant time we should have spent there!

"You shall not be jealous of Mr. Payne.[2] Remember he did Charles and I good service without grudge or grumbling. Say to him how much I regret that we owe him unreturnable obligations; for I still have my old fear that we shall never see him again. I received great pleasure from seeing his two successful pieces. My love to your boy Kenney, my boy James,

[1] Louisa, or Lou-Lou, Ellen, Betsy, and Sophy were Mrs. Kenney's daughters by Holcroft. James, Teresa, Virginia, and Charles were the same lady's children by Kenney.

[2] John Howard Payne. See Hazlitt's edition of Correspondence, ii. 84 *et seqq.*

and all my dear girls, and also to Rose; I hope she still drinks wine with you. Thank Lou-Lou[1] for her little bit of letter. I am in a fearful hurry, or I would write to her. Tell my friend the Poetess that I expect some french verses from her shortly. I have shewn Betsy's and Sophy's letters to all who came near me, and they have been very much admired. Dear Fanny brought me the bag. Good soul you are to think of me! Manning[2] has promised to make Fanny a visit this morning, happy girl! Miss James[3] I often see, I think never without talking of you. Oh the dear long dreary Boulevards! how I do wish to be just now stepping out of a Cuckoo[4] into them!

"Farewel, old tried friend, may we meet again! Would you could bring your house with all its noisy inmates, and plant it, garden, gables and all, in the midst of Covent Garden.

"Yours ever most affectionately,

"M. LAMB.

"My best respects to your good neighbours."

[Endorsed]

Mrs. Kenney.

Miss Kelly's scrap, written very faintly across the outside of the sheet, runs as follows:—

[1] Louisa Holcroft married Dr. Badams, and secondly the Baron De Merger, of Plessis la Barbe, near Tours, where I visited them in or about 1855.

[2] The Manning, of course, of the Letters.

[3] The lady who took charge of Miss Lamb during her French trip.

[4] A diligence, so called, which used to ply between the Champs Elysées and St. Cloud, Versailles, &c.

"The real old original Fanny Kelly takes this opportunity of assuring Mrs. Kenney that she remembers with pleasure them all, Oh, how imperfect is expression" [The rest, through the faint ink employed and the creasing of the paper, has become illegible; but the substance is that Miss Kelly hoped soon to have an opportunity of squeezing Mrs. Kenney's hand, and shewing her respectful and grateful attachment.]

Patmore, in his *Rejected Articles*, 1826, begins with An Unsentimental Journey, by Elia, which is nothing more than a fabrication by himself, based on his own experiences of French hotels and localities. He does not even mention that Lamb had a companion on his trip, and several friends at Paris and other points.

XXXII

Here is another long one to the Kenneys from Lamb himself, of the Anglo-Gallic epoch:

Charles Lamb to the Kenneys.

Lonres, October month, 1826.

"Dear Friends,—It is with infinite regret I inform you that the pleasing privilege of receiving Letters, by which I have for these twenty years gratified my friends and abused the liberality of the Company trading to the Orient, is now at an end. A cruel edict of the Directors has swept it away altogether. The devil sweep away their patronage also. Rascals, who think nothing of spunging on their employers for their venison and Turtle and Burgundy five days in the week, to the tune of five thousand pounds a year, now find out that the profits of trade will not allow the innocent communications of thought between their underlings and their friends in distant provinces to proceed untaxed, thus withering up the heart of friendship and making the news of a friend's good health worse than indifferent; a tidings to be deprecated as bringing with it ungracious influences. Adieu, gentle correspondents, kindly interchange of soul, interchange of love, of opinions, of puns, and what not. Henceforth, a friend that does not stand in visible or palpable distance to me is nothing to me. They have not left to the bosom of friendship even that cheap intercourse of sentiment—the twopenny medium. The upshot is you must not direct any more letters through me. To me you may annually or biennially transmit a brief account of your goings on, in single sheet, from which, after I have deducted as much as the postage comes to, the remainder will be pure pleasure. But no more of those pretty commissions and counter-commissions, orders & revoking of orders, obscure messages & obscurer explanations, by which the intellects of Marshall and Fanny used to be kept in a pleasing perplexity at the moderate cost of six or seven shillings a week. In short, you must use me no longer as a go-between. Henceforth I write up No Thoroughfare.

Well, and how far is Saint Wallery suer Some

from Paris, and do you get wine and walnuts tolerable, and the vintage, does it suffer from the wet. I take it the wine of this season will be all wine and water. And have you Plays and Green rooms, and Fanny Kellies to chat with of an evening, and is the air purer than the old gravel pits, and the bread so much whiter as they say? Lord, what things you see that travel. I daresay the people are all French, wherever you go; what an overwhelming effect that must have. I have stood one of 'em at a time, but two I generally found overpowring; but then in their own vineyards may be they [are] endurable enough. They say marmosets in Senegambia are as pleasant as the day's long, jumping and chattering in the orange twigs; but transport 'em one by one over here into England, they turn into monkeys, some with tails, some without, and are obliged to be kept in cages. I suppose you know we've left the Temple pro tempore. By the way, this conduct has caused many strange surmises in a good lady of our acquaintance. She lately sent for a young gentleman of the India House, who lives opposite her at Monroe's the flute shop in Skinner Street, Snowhill, — I mention no names. You shall never get out of me what lady I mean,—on purpose to ask all he knew about us. I had previously introduced him to her whist table. Her enquiries embraced every possible thing that could be known of me – how I stood in the India House, what was the amount of my salary, what it was likely to be hereafter, whether I was thought clever in business, why I had taken country lodgings, why at Kingsland in particular, had I friends in that road, was anybody expected to visit me, did I wish for visitors, would an unexpected call be gratifying or not, would it be better that she sent beforehand, did any body come to see me, was not there a gentleman of the name of Morgan, did he know him, did'nt he come to see me, did he know how Mr. Morgan lived, she could never make out how they were maintained, was it true he lived out of the profits of a linen draper's shop in Bishopsgate Street? (There she is a little right & a little wrong. M. is a Gentleman tobacconist). In short, she multiplied demands upon him till my friend, who is neither over modest nor nervous, declared he quite shuddered after laying me as bare to her curiosity as an anatomy. He trembled to think what she would ask next, my pursuits, inclinations, aversions, attachments (some, my dear friends, of a most delicate nature), she lugged 'em out of him, or would, had he been privy to them, as you pluck a horse bean from its iron stem, not as such tender rosebuds should be pulled. The fact is, I am come to Kingsland . . . and that is the truth of the matter; and nobody but yourselves should have extorted such a confession from me. I suppose you have seen by the Papers that Manning is arrived in England He expressed much mortification at not finding Mrs. Kenney in England. He looks a good deal sunburnt, and is got a little reserved, but I hope it will wear off. You will see by the Papers also that Dawe is Knighted. He has been painting the Princess of Coborg & her husband. This is all the news I could think of. Write to us, but not *by* us, for I have near ten correspondents of this latter description, and one or other comes pouring in every day, till my purse strings and heart strings crack. Bad habits are not all broken at once. I am sure that you will excuse the apparent indelicacy of mentioning this, but dear is my shirt but dearer is my skin, and 'tis too late when the steed is stole, to shut the stable door.

Well, and does Louisa grown [*sic*] a fine girl, is she likely to have her mother's complexion, and does Tom Polish in French air?—Henry I mean—and Kenney is-not so fidgety. YOU sit down sometimes for a quiet half hour or so, and all is comfortable, no bills (that you call writs), nor anything else (that you are equally sure to miss-call), to annoy you. Vive la gaite de cœur et la bell pastime, vive la beau France et revive mon cher Empreur.

"C. Lamb."

[Endorsed]
Mr. Kenney,
Saint Valery sur Somme,
France.

THE WILLIAMS CORRESPONDENCE

I now approach a remarkable series of letters sent by Lamb to Mrs. Williams, wife of the Rev. Mr. Williams, rector of Fornham, near Bury St. Edmunds. In the printed collections which have been so far given to the public, the correspondence with Mrs. Williams is limited to two letters, of which one has never yet been presented in its integrity. I was enabled by the kindness of that lady's grandson and representative, Mr. Cecil Turner, to increase the series to seven, and at the same time to supply the omitted passages in that of April 2, 1830.

But there were unquestionably other communications, now irretrievably lost, both before and after the dates of those which are preserved. We must rest and be thankful. The enrichment of the existing store is equally fortuitous and acceptable.

So far back as 1822, Crabb Robinson, who was himself an East Anglian, and who had relatives whom he frequently visited at Bury, gave the Lambs an introduction to Miss Williams,—probably related to the rector of Fornham, perhaps his sister,—just prior to their departure on their French trip; but it was a different Mrs. Williams, whom Alsop once met, with Mrs. Shelley, at Colebrooke Cottage, Islington. We hear nothing farther of any intercourse between the families, till we find Emma Isola established as a governess to the rector's daughters in 1830.

A good deal of information about this young lady, whom the Lambs adopted, occurs in the biographies and letters; and it is well known that she was the daughter of Carlo Isola, an Italian professor at Cambridge; but I do not recollect to have seen it anywhere mentioned that she was, no doubt, the grand-daughter of Agostino Isola, who brought out at Cambridge in 1786 an edition of Tasso, and whom his son may have succeeded in his educational functions at the University.

Was it in Agostino Isola's edition that the Lambs read the poet,—for Miss Lamb, at least, had made an attempt to learn Italian,—or in Fairfax's English version, an old acquaintance? For Lamb notes the purchase of a copy in a letter of 1797 to Coleridge, and calls upon him to rejoice with him at the piece of good fortune.

Emma Isola had gone down to Fornham to discharge her duties as governess in the house of Mrs. Williams, and was taken ill. On the 21st February, 1830, Lamb writes from Enfield to Moxon:

"A letter has just come from Mrs. Wms. to say that Emma is so poorly that she must have long holydays here. It has agitated me so much, and we shall expect her so hourly, that you shall excuse me to Wordsth for not coming up, we are both nervous and poorly."

Of course this letter from Fornham has shared

the doom of all but a fraction of Lamb's papers of the kind; but on the 26th he wrote to Mrs. Williams the first of the group which succeeds:

XXXIII

C. Lamb to Mrs. Williams.

[February 26, 1830.]

"Dear Madam,—May God bless you for your attention to our poor Emma! I am so shaken with your sad news I can scarce write. She is too ill to be removed at present; but we can only say that if she is spared, when that can be practicable, we have always a home for her. Speak to her of it, when she is capable of understanding, and let me conjure you to let us know from day to day, the state she is in. But one line is all we crave. Nothing we can do for her, that shall not be done. We shall be in the terriblest suspense. We had no notion she was going to be ill. A line from anybody in your house will much oblige us. I feel for the situation this trouble places you in.

Can I go to her aunt, or do anything? I do not know what to offer. We are in great distress. Pray relieve us, if you can, by somehow letting us know. I will fetch her here, or anything. Your kindness can never be forgot. Pray excuse my abruptness. I hardly know what I write. And take our warmest thanks. Hoping to hear something, I remain, dear Madam,

"Yours most faithfully,

"C. LAMB.

"Our grateful respects to Mr. Williams."

This singular letter betrays the passionate concern felt by the brother and sister for the young lady of their adoption, and places us in full inferential possession of the gravity of the illness by which Miss Isola had been so unexpectedly overtaken. It was an attack of brain fever.

XXXIV

To the Same.

"Enfield, 1 March, 1830.

"Dear Madam,—We cannot thank you enough. Your two words 'much better' were so considerate and good. The good news affected my sister to an agony of tears; but they have relieved us from such a weight. We were ready to expect the worst, and were hardly able to bear the good hearing. You speak so kindly of her, too, and think she may be able to resume her duties. We were prepared, as far as our humble means would have enabled us, to have taken her from all duties. But, far better for the dear girl it is that she should have a prospect of being useful.

"I am sure you will pardon my writing again; for my heart is so full, that it was impossible to refrain. Many thanks for your offer to write again, should any change take place. I dare not yet be quite out of fear, the alteration has been so sudden. But I will hope you will have a respite from the trouble of writing again. I know no expression to convey a sense of your kindness. We were in such a state expecting the post. I had almost resolved to come as near you as Bury; but my sister's health does not permit my absence on melancholy occasions. But, O, how happy will she be to part with me, when I shall hear the agreeable news that I may come and fetch her. She shall be as quiet as possible. No restorative means shall be wanting to restore her back to you well and comfortable.

"She will make up for this sad interruption of her young friend's studies. I am sure she will—she must—after you have spared her for a little time. Change of scene may do very much for her. I think this last proof of your kindness to her in her desolate state can hardly make her love and respect you more than she has ever done. O, how glad shall we be to return her fit for her occupation. Madam, I trouble you with my nonsense; but you would forgive me, if you knew how light-hearted you have made two poor souls at Enfield, that were gasping for news of their poor friend. I will pray for you and Mr. Williams. Give our very best respects to him, and accept our thanks. We are happier than we hardly know how to bear. God bless you! My very kindest congratulations to Miss Humphreys.[1]

"Believe me, dear Madam,

"Your ever obliged servant,

"C. LAMB."

It must be admitted that this unpublished

[1] There is, I believe, a letter from Lamb to Miss Humphreys extant; but I have not yet been able to see it. Miss Humphreys was apparently at Fornham Rectory, and the letter to her, if so, belongs no doubt to the present group.

matter, as it proceeds, is of very peculiar interest. The whole mind of the writer is irresistibly concentrated on a single point. He has cast aside all thought for things indifferent and external, and all power and desire to indulge in any allusions of a playful, much less jocose, character. The force of his mind was so thoroughly absorbed by this sorrow, that if early relief had not arrived by the convalescence of the invalid, the most serious effects might have followed.

XXXV

To the Same.

"Enfield, 5 Mar., 1830.

"Dear Madam,—I feel greatly obliged by your letter of Tuesday, and should not have troubled you again so soon, but that you express a wish to hear that our anxiety was relieved by the assurances in it. You have indeed given us much comfort respecting our young friend, but considerable uneasiness respecting your own health and spirits, which must have suffered under such attention. Pray believe me that we shall wait in quiet hope for the time, when I shall receive the welcome summons to come and relieve you from a charge, which you have executed with such tenderness. We desire nothing so much as to exchange it with you. Nothing shall be wanting on my part to remove her with the best judgment I can without (I hope) any necessity for depriving you of the services of your valuable housekeeper. Until the day comes, we entreat that you will spare yourself the trouble of writing, which we should be ashamed to impose upon you in your present weak state. Not hearing from you, we shall be satisfied in believing that there has been no relapse. Therefore we beg that you will not add to your troubles by unnecessary, though *most kind*, correspondence. Till I have the pleasure of thanking you personally, I beg you to accept these written acknowledgments of all your kindness. With respects to Mr. Williams and sincere prayers for both your healths, I remain,

"Your ever obliged servant,

"C. LAMB.

"My sister joins me in respects and thanks."

From this third letter we collect that Mrs. Williams had overtaxed her strength in nursing her patient. Miss Isola was steadily rallying; but these communications from Lamb, we must recollect, arrived at very short intervals. Upward of a fortnight, however, intervened before another letter from Lamb apprises us that Mrs. Williams now gave him and Miss Lamb hope that they might soon expect to be able to remove Miss Isola to Enfield.

XXXVI

To the Same.

"Dear Madam,—Once more I have to return you thanks for a very kind letter. It has gladdened us very much to hear that we may have hope to see our young friend so soon, and through your kind nursing so well recovered. I sincerely hope that your own health and spirits will not have been shaken: you have had a sore trial indeed, and greatly do we feel indebted to you for all which you have undergone. If I hear nothing from you in the mean time, I shall secure myself a place in the Cornwallis Coach for Monday. It will not be at all necessary that I shall be met at Bury, as I can well find my way to the Rectory, and I beg that you will **not** inconvenience yourselves by such attention. Accordingly as I find Miss Isola able to bear the journey, I intend to take the care of her by the same stage or by chaises perhaps, dividing the journey; but exactly as you shall judge fit. It is our misfortune that long journeys do not agree with my sister, who would else have taken this care upon herself, perhaps more properly. It is quite out of the question to rob you of the services of any of your domestics. I cannot think of it. But if in your opinion a female attendant would be requisite on the journey, and if you or Mr. Williams would feel *more comfortable* by her being in charge of two, I will most gladly engage one of her nurses or any young person near you, that you can recommend; for my object is to remove her in the way that shall be most satisfactory to yourselves.

"On the subject of the young people that you are interesting yourselves about, I will have the pleasure to talk to you, when I shall see you. I live almost out of the world and out of the sphere of being useful; but no pains of mine shall be spared, if but a prospect opens of doing a service. Could I do all I wish, and I indeed have grown helpless to myself and others, it must not satisfy the arrears of obligation I owe to Mr. Williams and yourself for all your kindness.

"I beg you will turn in your mind and consider in what most comfortable way Miss Isola can leave your house, and I will implicitly follow your suggestions. What you have done for her can never be effaced from our memories, and I would have you part with her in the way that would best satisfy yourselves.

"I am afraid of impertinently extending my letter, else I feel I have not said half what I would say. So, dear madam, till I have the pleasure of seeing you both, of whose kindness I have heard so much before, I respectfully take my leave with our kindest love to your poor patient and most sincere regards for the health and happiness of Mr. Williams and yourself. May God bless you.

"CH. LAMB.

"Enfield, Monday, 22 March."

The four letters which have gone before harp almost exclusively on one string; but they are of special value, since they exhibit the writer in the light nearest to that of a fond and anxious parent that he could ever expect to attain, and so far the present series, hitherto almost unknown, may be said to stand quite by itself.

The worst was over. Miss Isola was conveyed safely back to Enfield by her affectionate guardian, and the next letter reported her arrival and condition after the journey. It has been repeatedly printed, and may be found in Canon Ainger's collection.

I repeat that Mr. Cecil Turner furnished me in the most polite manner with this valuable information many years since, but I have not hitherto had an opportunity of utilizing it, and of publicly thanking him.

XXXVII*

To the Same.[1]

"Enfield, April 2, 1830.

"Dear Madam,—I have great pleasure in letting you know Miss Isola has suffered very little from fatigue on her long journey. I am ashamed to say that I came home rather the more tired of the two, but I am a very unpractised traveller. She has had two tolerable nights' sleep since, and is decidedly not worse[2] than when we left you. I remembered the magnesia according to your directions, & promise that she shall be kept very quiet, never forgetting that she is still an invalid. We found my sister very well in health, only a little impatient to see her; and, after a few hysterical tears for gladness, all was comfortable again. We arrived from Epping between

[1] Now first completely printed from the autograph.

[2] I am rather uncertain about this word; the transcript is on tracing paper, and is here and there rather indistinct.

five and six. The accidents of our journey were trifling, but you bade me tell them. We had then in the coach a rather talkative gentleman, but very civil all the way, and took up a servant maid at Stanford, going to a sick mistress. To the latter a participation in the hospitalities of your nice rusks and sandwiches proved agreeable, as it did to my companion, who took merely a sip of the weakest wine and water with them. The former engaged in a discourse for full twenty minutes on the probable advantages of steam carriages, which being merely problematical I bore my part in with some credit, in spite of my totally unengineer-like faculties. But when somewhere about Stanstead he put an unfortunate question to me as to the probability of its turning out a good turnip season, and when I, who am still [less] of an agriculturist than a steam philosopher, not knowing a turnip from a potato ground, innocently made answer that I believed it depended very much upon boiled legs of mutton, my unlucky reply set Miss Isola a laughing to a degree that disturbed her tranquility for the only moment in our journey. I am afraid my credit sank very low with my other fellow-traveller, who had thought he had met with a well-informed passenger, which is an accident so desirable in a stage-coach. We were rather less communicative, but still friendly, the rest of the way.

How I employed myself between Epping and Enfield the poor verses in the front of my paper[1] may inform you, which you may please to christen an Acrostic in a Cross Road, and which I

[1] See the Acrostics now first published, *post*.

wish were worthier of the lady they refer to; but I trust you will plead my pardon to her on a subject so delicate as a lady's good *name*. Your candour must acknowledge that they are written straight. And now, dear Madam, I have left myself hardly space to express my sense of the friendly reception I found at Fornham. Mr. Williams will tell you that we had the pleasure of a slight meeting with him on the road, where I could almost have told him, but that it seemed ungracious, that such had been your hospitality that I scarcely missed the good master of the family at Fornham, though heartily I should have rejoiced to have made a little longer acquaintance with him. I will say nothing of our deeper obligations to both of you, because I think that we agreed at Fornham that gratitude may be over-exacted on the part of the obliging, and over-expressed on the part of the obliged, person.

My sister and Miss Isola join in respects to Mr. Williams and yourself, and I beg to be remembered kindly to the Miss Hammonds[1] and the two Gentlemen whom I had the good fortune to meet at your house. I have not forgotten the election[2] in which you are interesting yourself, and the little that I can I will do.

Miss Isola will have the pleasure of writing to you next week, and we shall hope, at your leisure, to hear of your own health, &c. I am, dear madam, with great respect, your obliged,

"CHARLES LAMB."

[1] Probably of Woodbridge.

[2] The case, to which Lamb refers in the letter of March 22.

On the back of this letter occur a few lines in Miss Isola's hand, as follow:—

"I must just add a line to beg you will let us hear from you, my dear Mrs. Williams. I have just received the forwarded letter [from] Fornham. We have talked about you constantly, and I felt strange at this home the first day" [the rest is unintelligible].

One more letter, about two weeks later, completes the series, so far as it is my power to complete it. The epistle now to be given accompanied the "Acrostic to a Young Lady, who desired me to write her epitaph."

XXXVIII

To the Same.

"Enfield, Tuesday [April 21, 1830].

"Dear Madam,—I have ventured upon some lines, which combine my old acrostic talent (which you first found out) with my new profession of epitaph-monger. As you did not please to say, when you would die, I have left a blank space for the date. May kind heaven be a long time in filling it up. At least you cannot say that these lines are not about you, though not much to the purpose. We were very sorry to hear that you have not been very well, and hope that a little excursion may revive you. Miss Isola is thankful for her added day; but I verily think she longs to see her young friends once more, and will regret less than ever the end of her holydays. She cannot be going on more quietly than she is doing here, and you will perceive amendment.

"I hope all her little commissions will all be brought home to your satisfaction. When she returns, we purpose seeing her to Epping on her journey. We have had our proportion of fine weather and some pleasant walks, and she is stronger, her appetite good, but less wolfish than at first, which we hold a good sign. I hope Mr. Wing will approve of its abatement. She desires her very kindest respects to Mr. Williams and yourself, and wishes to rejoin you. My sister and myself join in respect, and pray tell Mr. Donne, with our compliments, that we shall be disappointed, if we do not see him.

"This letter being very neatly written, I am very unwilling that Emma should club any of her disproportionate scrawl to deface it.

"Your obliged servant,

"C. Lamb."

Mrs. Williams,
W. B. Donne, Esq.,
Matteshall, East Dereham,
Norfolk.

The Mr. Donne mentioned by Lamb was the late William Bodham Donne, Deputy Licenser of Plays, and at one period Secretary to the London Library.

Miss Isola did return to Fornham, and was there on the 28th June, 1830, when Lamb, writing to Bernard Barton, says:—

"You will see that I am worn to the poetical dregs, condescending to acrostics, which are nine fathoms beneath album verses; but they were written at the request of the lady, where our Emma is."

But I am informed that she did not remain long, though the reason of her final relinquishment of the duties is not specified.

Lamb is found below introducing to his official friend in Thiefland an acquaintance of the Whites—not James White, but Edward of the India House. He mentions Leigh Hunt and the *Examiner*.

XXXIX

To Barron Field.

"London, 16 Aug., 1820.

"Dear Field,—Captain Ogilvie, who conveys this note to you, and is now paying for the first time a visit to your remote shores, is the brother of a Gentleman intimately connected with the family of the *Whites*, I mean of Bishopsgate Street—and you will much oblige them and myself by any service or civilities you can shew him.

"I do not mean this for an answer to your warm-hearted Epistle, which demands ahd shall have a much fuller return. We receiped your Australian First Fruits, of which I shall say nothing here, but refer you to . . . [? Hunt] of the *Examiner*, who speaks our mind on all public subjects. I can only assure you that both Coleridge and Wordsworth, and also C. Lloyd, who has lately reappeared in the poetical horizon, were hugely taken with your Kangaroo.

"When do you come back full of riches and renown, with the regret of all the honest, and all the other part of the colony? Mary swears she shall live to see it.

"Pray are you King's or Queen's men in Sidney? Or have thieves no politics? Man, don't let this lie about your room for your bed sweeper or Major Domo to see, he mayn't like the last paragraph.

"This is a dull and lifeless scroll. You shall have soon a tissue of truth & fiction impossible to be extricated, the interleavings shall be so delicate, the partitions perfectly envisible [? indivisible], it shall puzzle you till you return, & [then I will not explain it. Till then a . . . adieu, with kind rem^brces of me both to you & . . . [Signature and a few words torn off.]

"B. Field, Esq."

[Endorsed]

Barron Field, Esqr.

By favor of Captn Ogilvie.

The connection of Lamb with the *London Magazine* (it is stated by Talfourd, through the introduction of Hazlitt) brought him into contact with John Scott, the accomplished and ill-fated editor of that periodical. The few lines below allude to some trifling contribution for the Poets' Corner.

XL

To John Scott.

"Dr Sir,—I sent you yesterday by the 2d post 2 small copies of verses direct[d] by mistake to N. 8 York St. if you have *not* rec[d] them, pray favor me with a line. From your not writing, I shall conclude you have got them.

"Yours resp[fly]

"C. LAMB.

"Thursday 24 Aug. 20. E. I. H."

[Endorsed]

J. Scott Esqr.,
4 York Street Cov[t] Garden.

XLI

To John Taylor.

"July 21, 1821.

"Dr. Sir,—The *Lond. Mag.* is chiefly pleasant to me, because some of my friends write in it. I hope Hazlitt intends to go on with it, we cannot spare Table Talk. For myself I feel almost exhausted, but I will try my hand a little longer, and shall not at all events be written out of it by newspaper paragraphs. Your proofs do not seem to want my helping hand, they are quite correct always. For God's sake change *Sisera* to *Jael*. This last paper will be a choke-pear I fear to some people, but as you do not object to it, I can be under little apprehension of your exerting your Censorship too rigidly.

"Thanking you for your extract from M[r] E.'s letter,
"I remain, D[r] Sir,
"Your obliged,
"C. Lamb.

"Mess[rs] Taylor & Hessey,
Booksellers,
Fleet Street.
"M[r] Taylor."

Canon Ainger and myself print two letters from Lamb to William Harrison Ainsworth, at the time a mere youth, but beginning to interest himself in literary matters. They are dated respectively December 9 and 29, 1823; it may be pointed out that the Warner received as a book offered for Lamb's acceptance, and eventually retained by him, was a poetical volume entitled *Syrinx*, 1597, by that writer, and not, as has always been imagined, his *Albion's England*. The copy which belonged to Lamb is now in the Dyce Collection.

The two letters in question are incorrectly given by me, who am followed by the Canon as usual; but the divergences are not vital. Lamb himself misquotes Marlowe. Both the letters are directed to Ainsworth at King Street, Manchester.

But the acquaintance with Ainsworth had commenced some time before the unpublished letter, which I shall presently give, and which goes back to the May of 1822; for then Lamb had lent his Manchester correspondent a copy of Cyril Tourneur's play or plays, in which Ainsworth must have shown his interest. Doubtless several letters have to be recovered, or are lost. Altogether, the one here printed is as interesting as the couple in type.

A good deal of interest still survives in the author of *Rookwood.* My father used to relate a personal trait of him, when he had friends to dinner. He locked his outside gate at the stroke of the clock, and no late comer was admitted.

XLII

To William Harrison Ainsworth.

"Dear Sir,—I have read your poetry with pleasure. The tales are pretty and prettily told, the language often finely poetical. It is only sometimes a little careless, I mean as to redundancy. I have marked certain passages (in pencil only, which will easily obliterate) for your consideration. Excuse this liberty. For the distinction you offer me of a dedication, I feel the honor of it, but I do not think it would advantage the publication. I am hardly on an eminence enough to warrant it. The Reviewers, who are no friends of mine—the two big ones especially who make a point of taking no notice of anything I bring out—may take occasion by it to decry us both. But I leave you to your own judgment. Perhaps, if you wish to give me a kind word, it will be more appropriate *before your republication of Tourneur*.

"The 'Specimens' would give a handle to it, which the poems might seem to want. But I submit it to yourself with the old recollection that 'beggars should not be chusers' and remain with great respect and wishing success to both your publications

"Your obet Sert

"C. Lamb.

"No hurry at all for Tourneur.[1]

"Tuesday 7 May '22."

[Endorsed]

W. H. Ainsworth Esq.

XLIII

To Thomas Hardy.

"Dear Sir,—Miss Hazlitt[2] has begged me to say to you that the novel, which you kindly promised to introduce to Mr. Ridgway, is lying for that purpose at Mr. Hone's, Ludgate Street, where you will perhaps be so kind as to send for it. She is going on 10th May as Governess into the family of Mrs. Brookes, Dawlish, where she shall be thankful to receive any communi-

[1] This is the only intimation, I believe, that Ainsworth projected a reprint of Tourneur's play or plays.

[2] Mary, daughter of the miniature-painter.

cations respecting the novel. She is now at 14, Queen's Square, Bristol.

"I am, Sir,
"With great respect,
"Yours, &c.,
"CH. LAMB.

"India House,
"24 Apr. 1824."
[Endorsed:]
Mr. Hardy,
30 Queen's Square,
Pimlico.

XLIV*

To Miss Hutchinson.

"Desk, 11 Nov., 1825.

"My Dear Miss Hutchinson,—Mary bids me thank you for your kind letter. We are a little puzzled about your whereabouts. Miss Wordsworth writes Torkay, and you have queerly made it Torquay. Now Tokay we have heard of, and Torbay, which we take to be the true *male* spelling of the place; but somewhere we fancy it to be on 'Devon's leafy shores,' where we heartily wish the kindly breezes may restore all that is invalid among you. Robinson is returned, and speaks much of you all. We shall be most glad to hear good news from you from time to time. The best is, Procter is at last married. We have made sundry attempts to see the bride, but have accidentally failed, she being gone out a gadding. We had promised our dear friends the Monkhouses—promised ourselves rather—a visit to them at Ramsgate; but I thought it best, and Mary seemed to have it at heart too, not to go far from home these last holydays. It is connected with a sense of unsettlement, and secretly I know she hoped that such abstinence would be friendly to her health. She certainly has escaped her sad yearly visitation, whether in consequence of it, or of faith in it, and we have to be thankful for a good 1824. To get such a notion into our heads may go a great way another year. Not that we quite confined ourselves; but assuming Islington to be head quarters, we made timid flights to Ware, Watford, &c., to try how the trouts tasted, for a night out or so, not long enough to make the sense of change oppressive, but sufficient to scour the rust of home. Coleridge is not returned from the sea. As a little scandal may divert you recluses, we were in the Summer dining at a clergyman of Southey's "Church of England," at Hertford, the same who officiated to Thurtell's last moments, and indeed an old contemporary Blue of C.'s and mine at school. After dinner we talked of C.; and F., who is a mighty good fellow in the main, but hath his cassock prejudices, inveighed against the moral character of C. I endeavoured to enlighten him on the subject, till having driven him out of some of his holds, he stopped my mouth at once by appealing to me whether it was not very well known that C. "at that very moment was living in a state of open adultery with Mrs. I * * * * * * at Highgate?" Nothing I could say, serious or bantering, after that, could remove the deep inrooted conviction of the whole company assembled that such was the case! Of course you will keep this quite close, for I would not involve my poor blundering friend, who I dare say believed it all thoroughly. My interference of course was imputed to the goodness of my heart, that could imagine nothing wrong, &c. Such it is if ladies will go gadding about with other people's husbands at watering places. How careful we should be to avoid the appearance of evil!

"I thought this anecdote might amuse you. It is not worth resenting seriously; only I give it as a specimen of orthodox candour. O Southey, Southey, how long would it be before you would find one of us Unitarians propagating such unwarrantable scandal! Providence keep you all from the foul fiend, scandal, and send you back well and happy to dear Gloster Place!

"C. L.

"Miss Hutchinson,
"T. Monkhouse, Esq.,
"Strand, Torkay, Torbay, Devon.

XLV

To B. W. Procter.

[No date or postmark.]

"Dear P,—We shall be most glad to see you, though more glad to have seen double *you*, but we will expect finer walking-weather. Bring my *Congreve*, 2[d] vol., in your hand. I have 2 books of yours lock'd up, but how shall I tell it, *horresco referens*, that I miss, and can't possibly account for it, *Hollis on Johnson's Milton!* I will march the town thro', but I will repair the loss. You will be sorry to hear that poor Monkhouse died on Saturd[y] at Clifton.

"C. L."

XLVI

To Charles Ollier.

"Dear O.,—I send you 8 more jests, with the terms which my friend asks, which you will be so kind as to get an answer to from Colburn, that I may tell him whether to go on with them. You will see his short note to me at the end, and tear it off. It is not for me to judge, but, considering the scarceness of the materials, what he asks is, I think, mighty reasonable, *Do not let him be even known as a friend of mine.* You see what he says about 5 going in first as a trial, but these will make 13 in all. Tell me by what time he need send more, I suppose not for some time (if you do not bring 'em out this month).

"Keep a place for me till the middle of the month, for I cannot hit on anything yet. I meant nothing by my crochets but extreme difficulty in writing. But I will go on as long as I can.

"C. LAMB."

[Endorsed]

Mr. Ollier,
Mr. Colburn's,
New Burlington Street.

[Postmarked]

Jan. 25 [?], 1826.

XLVII

To the Same. [? 1826.]

"Dr O.,—We dine at 4 on Monday. As I expect the Authoress to tea, pray have a bit of opinion to give on her Manuscript, or she will haunt me. Could you let me have the last Magazine I wrote in, & which I had not about July or August last, containing the Essay on Sulkiness, being the last of the Popular Fallacies. Till I see you. A-Dieu

"C. LAMB.

"Saty"

For Mr. Ollier, at Mr. Colburn's,
Burlingtn Street.

The next item is addressed to an hitherto unknown correspondent, and from the tone we are perhaps justified in concluding that the recipient was a person at whose house the Lambs occasionally stayed, when in town, at this period.

XLVIII

To Mrs. Dillon.

[Postmarked] July 21, 1827.

"I think it is not quite the etiquette for me to answer my sister's letter, but she is no great scribe, and I know will be glad to find it done for her. We are both very thankful to you for your thinking about Emma, whom for the last seven weeks I have been teaching Latin, &

she is already qualified to impart the rudiments to a child. We shall have much pleasure in seeing Mr. Dillon & you again, but I don't know when that may be, as we find ourselves very comfortable at Enfield.

"My sister joins in acknowledgments, & kindest respects to Mr. Dillon & yourself.

"Your obliged,

"C. LAMB.

"Enfield."

[Endorsed]

Mrs. Dillon,
8, Fitzroy Street,
Fitzroy Square,
London.

There now comes a little batch of Enfield letters to Hood, Cowden Clarke, and Hone. Those to Hood are on the death of his infant daughter, and in relation to an expected visit from his wife and himself.

In the *Gem* for 1829 Hood printed the verses by Lamb, which in the original manuscript occupy two pages and a half of quarto paper, and were posted by him to the bereaved father on the 30th of May, 1827. They are headed, "On an Infant Dying as soon as born," and are directed to "T. Hood, Esqr., 2, Robert Street, Adelphi."

It is very striking that Lamb, in his letter of condolence, cannot withstand the temptation not merely of making a pun, but of confessing that he had laid a sixpenny wager with Moxon as to the sex of the poor little creature.

XLIX

To Thomas Hood.

[May, 1827.]

"Dearest Hood,—Your news has spoil'd us a merry meeting. Miss Kelly and we were coming, but your letter elicited a flood of tears from Mary, and I saw she was not fit for a party. God bless you and the mother (or should be mother) of your sweet girl that should have been. I have won sexpence of Moxon by the *sex* of the dear gone one.

"Yours most truly and hers,

"C. L."

L

To the Same.

[No date.]

"Dear Hood,—We will look out for you on Wednesday, be sure, tho we have not eyes like Emma, who, when I made her sit with her back to the window to keep her to her Latin, literally saw round backwards every one that past, and, O, she were here to jump up and shriek out 'There are the Hoods!' We have had two pretty letters from her, which I long to show you—together with Enfield in her May beauty.

"Loves to Jane."[1]

[Here follow rough caricatures of Charles and his sister, and "I can't draw no better."]

[1] Mrs. Hood, sister of John Hamilton Reynolds.

LI

To Charles Cowden Clarke.

"Dear C.,—I shall do very well. The sunshine is medicinal, as you will find when you venture hither some fine day. Enfield is beautiful.

"Yours truly,

"C. L."

Of a letter to Hone respecting the Every Day Book, which the author forwarded to Lamb in numbers, a portion has been given by the present writer; but the entire text is now first printed. There is no difficulty in believing that the goodness of the Lambs to Hone, and the interest which they awakened in others on his behalf, were of vital service to that estimable and unfortunate man.

LII

To William Hone.

[August 12, 1825.]

"Dear Hone,—Your books are right acceptable. I did not enter further about Dogget, because on 2d thoughts the Book I mean does not refer to him. A coach from Bell or Bell and Crown sets of to Enfield at ½ past 4. Put yourself in it tomorrow afternoon, and come to us. We desire to shew you the country here. If we are out, when you come, the maid is instructed to keep you upon tea and proper bread and butter till we come home. Pray secure me the last No. of Every day book, that which has S. R[ay] in it, which by mistake has never come. Did our newsman not bring it on Monday? Don't send home for it, for if I get it hereafter (so I have it at last) it is all I want. Mind, we shall expect you Saty night or Sundy morning. There are Edmonton coaches from Bishopsgte every half hour, the walk thence to Enfield easy across the fields, a mile and half.

"Yours truly,

"C. LAMB.

"This invitation is 'ingenuous.' I assure you we want to see you here. Or will Sundy night and all day Monday suit you better?

"The coach sets you down at Mrs. Leishman's.

"Friday."

As far back as April 3, 1828, Lamb had addressed from Enfield a letter of appeal to the Rev. Edward Irving, of which Hone was apparently the bearer. It is in the edition of the Letters by Canon Ainger, and I need not therefore do more than refer to it.

A couple of years later, with the assistance of friends, and principally of Lamb himself, doubtless, the Hone family had established a coffee-shop, The Grasshopper, in Gracechurch Street. In an inedited letter to Basil Montagu, May 10, 1830, poor Hone draws a dreadful picture of his financial and domestic condition. The friend referred to was, of course, Lamb, who had enlisted the sympathy and professional or official assistance of Montagu in the matter. Hone writes as follows to the Commissioner of Bankruptcy:—

"It may be easily conceived that since the day you kindly proffered me your aid if it were requisite in the Bankrupt's Court at Whitehall, I have not been 'tried with riches'—no one can imagine the distresses and heart sickenings I endured with my wife and eight children while we secretly struggled through a subsequent twelvemonth of concealed destitution. Literary employment was precarious; a friend advised and assisted in the taking of these premises, which he judiciously conceived might be opened as a respectable coffee house, under the management of my eldest daughter."

The next has not hitherto been printed. It refers to Matilda Hone's illness, to the Extracts from the Garrick Plays for the *Table Book*, and to Hone's straitening circumstances:

To the Same.

Enfield [August 10, 1827].

"My dear Hone,—We are both excessively grieved at poor Matilda's illness, whom we have ever regarded with the greatest respect. Pray God your next news, which we shall expect most anxiously, shall give hopes of her recovery. Mary keeps her health very well, and joins in kind rememb[ces] and best wishes.

"A few more numbers, about 7, will empty my Extract book, then we will consult about the Specimens; by then I hope you will be able to talk about business. How you continue your book at all and so well in trying circumst[ces] I know not. But don't let it stop. Would to God I could help you; but we have the house full of comp[y,] which we came to avoid.

"God bless you,

"C. L."

LI

To the Same.

[Postmarked] May 12, 1830.

"Dear H.,—I heard from Rogers that Southey, is, or is expected to be, in town. You may learn at my friend Rickman's in Palace yard. Go there. R. is one of my oldest friends.

"C. LAMB.

"R. lives next door to the Entrance to Westminst[r] Hall.

"M[r] Hone,

"13, Gracechurch Street."

"*Note on back ? in Hone's hand:* "Rickman, then 2[d] clerk at the table of the House of Commons. Mr. S. used, when in town, generally to remain at Mr. R.'s house."

LII

To the Same.

[Postmarked] July 1, 1830.

Pray let Matilda keep my Newspapers till you hear from me, as we are meditating a town residence. "C. LAMB.

"Let her keep them as the apple of her eye."

[Endorsed]

Mr. Hone,

13, Gracechurch Street.

I now return to Miss Lamb, and have the pleasure of inviting attention to an interesting and rather long letter by her, directed to the Hoods at Winchmore Hill, who had been staying under their roof at Enfield, and whom the writer was apprehensive of having somehow offended. Mrs. Paris, from Cambridge, had been paying a visit to the Lambs, and they had not only Emma Isola, but her sister Harriet, with them. Emma was expecting a summons to return to Fornham; Lamb was helping her to "rub up" her Latin.

LIII

Miss Lamb to the Hoods.

[Enfield, end of April, 1828].

"My dear Friends,—My brother and Emma are to send you a partnership letter, but as I have a great dislike to my stupid scrap at the fag end of a dull letter, and, as I am left alone, I will say my say first; and in the first place thank you for your kind letter; it was a mighty comfort to me. Ever since you left me, I have been thinking I know not what, but every possible thing that I could invent, why you should be angry with me for something I had done or left undone during your uncomfortable sojourn with us, and now I read your letter and think and feel all is well again. Emma and her sister Harriet are gone to Theobalds Park, and Charles is gone to Barnet to cure his headache, which a good old lady has talked him into. She came on Thursday and left us yesterday evening. I mean she was Mrs. Paris, with whom Emma's aunt lived at Cambridge, and she had so much to [tell] her about Cambridge friends, and to [tell] us about London ditto, that her tongue was never at rest though the whole day, and at night she took Hood's Whims and Oddities to bed with her and laught all night. Bless her spirits! I wish I had them and she were as mopey as I am. Emma came on Monday, and the week has passed away I know not how. But we have promised all the week that we should go and see the Picture friday or saturday, and stay a night or so with you. Friday came and we could not turn Mrs. Paris out so soon, and on friday evening the thing was wholly given up. Saturday morning brought fresh hopes; Mrs. Paris agreed to go to see the picture with us, and we were to walk to Edmonton. My Hat and my *new gown* were put on in great haste, and his honor, who decides all things here, would have it that we could not get to Edmonton in time; and there was an end of all things. Expecting to see you, I did not write."

"Monday evening.

"Charles and Emma are taking a second walk. Harriet is gone home. Charles wishes to know more about the Widow. Is it to be made to match a drawing? If you could throw a little more light on the subject, I think he would do it, when Emma is gone; but his time will be quite taken up with her; for, besides refreshing her Latin, he gives her long lessons in arithmetic, which she is sadly deficient in. She leaves in a week, unless she receives a renewal of her holydays, which Mrs. Williams has half promised to send her. I do verily believe that I may hope to pass the last one, or two, or three nights with you, as she is to go from London to Bury. We will write to you the instant we receive Mrs. W.'s letter. As to my poor sonnet, and it is a very poor sonnet, only answered very well the purpose it was written for, Emma left it behind her, and nobody remembers more than one line of it, which is, I think, sufficient to convince you it would make no great impression in an Annual. So pray let it rest in peace, and I will make Charles write a better one instead.

"This shall go to the Post to-night. If any [one] chooses to add anything to it they may. It will glad my heart to see you again.

"Yours (both yours) truly and affectionately,

"M. Lamb.

"Becky is going by the Post office, so I will send it away. I mean to commence letter-writer to the family."

LIV

Charles Lamb to Miss James.

[Dec. 31, 1828.]

"We have just got your letter. I think Mother Reynolds will go on quietly, Mrs. Scrimpshaw having kittens. The name of the late Laureat was Henry James Pye, and when his 1st Birthday

Ode came out, which was very poor, somebody being ask'd his opinion of it said—

> And when the Pye was open'd,
> The birds began to sing,
> And was not this a dainty dish
> To set before the King?

"Pye was brother to old Major Pye, and father to Mrs. Arnold, and uncle to a General Pye, all friends of Miss Kelly. Pye succeeded Thos. Weston, Weston succeeded Wm. Whitehead, Whitehead succeeded Colly Cibber, Cibber succeeded Eusden, Eusden succeeded Thos. Shadwell, Shadwell succeeded Dryden, Dryden succeeded Davenant, Davenant succeeded God knows whom. There never was a Rogers a Poet Laureat, there is an old living Poet of that name, a Banker, as you know, author of the Pleasures of Memory, where Moxon goes to breakfast in a fine house in the Green Park, but he was never Laureat. Southey is the present one, & for anything I know or care Moxon may succeed him. We have a copy of 'Xmas' for you, so you may give your own to Mary as soon as you please. We think you need not have exhibited your mountain shyness before Mr. B. He is neither shy himself, nor patronizes it in others. So with many thanks Good Bye. Emma comes on Thursday.

"C. L."

"The Poet Laureat[1] whom Davenant succeeded was Rare Ben Jonson, who I believe was the first regular Laureat with the appointmt of

[1] On a separate slip of paper.

£100 a year & a Butt of Sack or Canary. So add that to my little list.

"C. L."

[Endorsed]

Miss James,
20, Upper Charles Street,
Paid. Goswell Street Road.

A short note to Coleridge supplies, if nothing else, a potent contrast to the letters of earlier years.

LV*

To S. T. Coleridge.

"13 April, 1831.

"Dear C.,—I am *daily* for this week expecting Wordsworth, who will not name a day. I have been expecting him by months and by weeks; but he has reduced the hope within the seven fractions hebdomidal of this hebdoma. Therefore I am sorry I cannot see you on Thursday. I think within a week or two I shall be able to invite myself some day for a day, but we hermits with difficulty poke out of our shells. Within that ostraceous retirement I meditate not unfrequently on you. My sister's kindest remembrances to your both.

"C. L."

Moxon having established a new venture, under the title of *The Englishman's Magazine*, in 1831, it almost necessarily became part of Lamb's duty to lend it a helping hand, which he did in certain papers headed "Peter's Net." This explains the signature.

LVI

To Edward Moxon.

[1831.]

"Dear M.,—I have ingeniously contrived to review myself.

"Tell me if this will do. Mind, for such things as these—half quotations—I do not charge *Elia* price. Let me hear of, if not see you.

"PETER."

[Endorsed]
Mr. Moxon,
Publisher,
64, New Bond Street,
London.

The next item was addressed to the daughters of Mr. Joseph Hume, at one time of Somerset House and of Bayswater, the common friend of Lamb and Hazlitt. Amelia Hume became Mrs. Bennett, Julia Mrs. Todhunter. The latter personally informed me in 1888 that her Aunt Augusta perfectly recollected all the circumstances. The incident seems to have taken place at the residence of Mr. Hume, in Percy Street, Bloomsbury, and it was Amelia who found the threepence-halfpenny in the coat which Lamb left behind him, and who repaired the button-holes. The sister who is described as "Scots wha ha'e" was Louisa Hume; it was a favourite song with her. These lines may be added to the series of light and jocose effusions already in print. The Gallicism carries evidence of them having been written posterior to the period of Lamb's return from his French trip in 1825. The recollection of the journey continued to linger for some time in the letters in the shape of scraps of the language of the country very much of the school of Stratford-at-Bow. Mrs. Todhunter supplies the exact date.

LVII

To the Misses Hume.

[1832.]

"Many thanks for the wrap-rascal, but how delicate the insinuating in, into the pocket, of that 3½*d*., in paper too! Who was it? Amelia, Caroline, Julia, Augusta, or 'Scots who have'?

"As a set-off to the very handsome present, which I shall lay out in a pot of ale certainly to *her* health, I have paid sixpence for the mend of two button-holes of the coat now return'd. She shall not have to say, 'I don't care a button for her.'

"Adieu, très aimables!

Buttons	6*d*.
Gift	3½
Due from ——	2½

which pray accept . . . from your foolish coat-forgetting "C. L."

In the following we too readily discern one of those intervals of depression which marked the closing years:

LVIII

To Edward Moxon.

[Postmarked] July 12, 1832.

"Dear M.,—My hand shakes so, I can hardly say don't come yet. I have been worse to-day than you saw me. I am going to try water gruel & quiet if I can get it. But a visitor hast [*sic*] just been down, & another a day or two before, & I feel half frantic. I will write when better. Make excuses to Foster [*sic*] for the present.

"C. Lamb.

"Mr. Moxon,
64, New Bond Street."

LIX

To Charles Ryle.[1]

[5 Nov., 1833].

"Dear Ryle,—Please to pay the Bearer *five shillings* on my account.

"Yours ever with loves at home,

"C. Lamb.

"To Chs Ryle, Esqre
"East India House."

[Endorsed]
Mr Gunston,
Spencer's Public Library,
314, Holborn.

LX

To Edward Moxon.

"Dear M.,—As I see no blood marks on the Green Lanes road, I conclude you got in safe

[1] Now first printed. Ryle was one of Lamb's executors, and the sole interest of the little note is, that it seems to be the only extant communication to him by his friend.

skins home. Have you thought of enquiring Miss Wilson's change of abode? Of the 2 copies of my Drama I want one sent to Wordsworth, together with a complete copy of Hone's Table Book, for which I shall be your debtor till we meet. Perhaps Longmans will take charge of this parcel. The other is for Coleridge, at Mr. Gilman's, Grove, Highgate, which may be sent, or, if you have a curiosity to see him, you will make an errand with it to him, & tell him we mean very soon to come & see him, if the Gilmans can give or get us a bed. I am ashamed to be so troublesome. Pray let Hood see the *Ecclectic Review*—a rogue!

"Yours truly,

"C. L.

"The 2d parts [*sic*] of the Blackwood you may make waste paper of."

[Endorsed]
E. Moxon, Esqre

LXI

To W. P. Sherlock.

[Postm. Nov. 15, 1834].

"Sir,—The picture you allude to is not in my possession. It was painted for Dr Stoddart, now in Malta.

"C. LAMB."

[Endorsed]
Mr W. P. Sherlock,
67 [obliterated by p.m.][1]

[1] Note in another, probably one of the Sherlocks' hand: "From C. Lamb [Elia] to W. P. Sherlock, who had applied to him for his Portrait painted by Hazlet." Probably the Macmillan copy.

LETTERS TO LAMB

LETTERS TO LAMB

So much has been said and written of the destruction by Lamb of all the communications addressed to him by friends, and notably by Coleridge (that early and life-long one), that I may perhaps be forgiven, if from the originals in my own hands I reproduce for the first time in an accurate form two of the four letters from Coleridge to Lamb at present extant, and one or two others similarly situated. The former occur in a manner which accounts for their preservation; for they are written on the fly-leaves of a copy of the *Works of Samuel Daniel*, 1718, which once belonged to ELIA, and was given by his sister, about fifty years ago, to the father of the present writer—the son of the Hazlitt whom Elia knew so well.

The copy of Daniel, which they accompany, is further enriched by copious MSS. notes in the hands of Coleridge himself and Lamb, and it is one of some dozen books, which, when the collection was purchased by a New York House in 1848, did not form part of the bargain, having been already distributed as souvenirs among the personal friends of the family. To speak the plain truth, the choicest portion of the library remained behind. Both letters are limited to literary criticism on the merits of Daniel in the eyes of the writer:—

Tuesday, Feb. 10, 1808.

"Dear Charles,—I think more highly, far more, of the 'Civil Wars' than you seemed to do on Monday night (Feb. 9th 1808). The verse does not teaze *me;* and all the while I am reading it I cannot but fancy a plain England-loving English Country Gentleman with only some dozen Books in his whole Library, and at a time when a 'Mercury' or 'Intelligencer' was seen by him once in a month or two, making this his Newspaper & political Bible at the same time, & reading it so often as to store his memory with its aphorisms. Conceive a good man of that time, diffident and passive, yet *rather* inclined to Jacobitism, seeing the reasons of the Revolutionary Party, yet by disposition and old principles leaning in quiet nods and sighs, at his own parlour fire, to the hereditary Right—(and of these characters there must have been many)—& then read the poems, assuming in your head his character—conceive how grave he would look, and what pleasure [there would be, what[1]] unconscious, harmless,

[1] Supplied in the handwriting of Lamb.

humble self-conceit, self-compliment in his gravity—how *wise* he would feel himself—& yet how forbearing, how much calmed by that most calming reflection (when it is really the mind's own reflection)—aye, it was just so in Henry the 6th's Time—always the same passions at work, &c. Have I injured thy book?—or wilt thou like it the better therefore? But I have done as I would gladly be done by—*thee* at least.

"S. T. COLERIDGE."

In estimating the remarks of Coleridge respecting Daniel it must, I think, occur to any one, that he has confounded the date of the particular edition employed with the period to which the poet belonged. Jacobitism and hereditary right were questions which had not arisen in the lifetime of Daniel. In compiling his metrical narrative of the Civil Wars of the Roses, he went, not to *Mercuries* and *Intelligencers*, because they did not exist, but to the Chronicles.

Second Letter. 5 hours after the first.

"Dear Charles,—You must read over these 'Civil Wars' again. We both know what a *mood* is, and the genial mood will, it shall, come for my sober-minded Daniel. He was a Tutor and a sort of steward in a noble Family, in which Form was religiously observed, and Religion formally, & yet there was such warm blood & mighty muscle of substance within, that the moulding views did not direct, tho' they stiffened the vital man within. Daniel caught & communicated the spirit of the great Countess of Pembroke, the glory of the North; he *formed* her mind, and her mind inspirited him. Gravely sober on all ordinary affairs, & not easily excited by any—yet there is one, on which his Blood boils—whenever he speaks of English valour exerted against a foreign Enemy. Do read over—but some evening when we are quite comfortable, at your fireside—and, O, where shall I ever be, if I am not so there?—that is, the last Altar, on the . . . of which my old Feelings hang; but, alas! listen & tremble—nonsense!—well I will read it to you & Mary, the 205th, 206th, and 207th page, above all that 93rd stanza—what is there in description superior even in Shakespere? only that Shakespere would have given one of his *Glows* to the first line, and flattered the mountain Top with his sovran Eye, instead of that poor 'a marvellous advantage of his Years.' But this, however, is Daniel; and he must not be read piecemeal. Even by leaving off & looking at a stanza by itself, I find the loss.

"S. T. COLERIDGE.

"O Charles! I am *very*, very ill. Vixi."

"And, in a different style, the 98th stanza, p. 208; & what an image in 107, p. 211![1] Thousands even of educated men would become more sensible, fitter to be members of Parliament, or Ministers, by reading Daniel—and even

[1] There are long MSS. notes by Coleridge at both these places.

those who *quoad intellectum* only gain refreshment of notions already their own, must become better Englishmen, & if not too late, write a kind note about him.

"S. T. Coleridge."

"Is it from any hobby-horsical love of our old writers (& of such a passion respecting Chaucer, Spenser, Ben Jonson's Poems, I have occasionally seen glaring proofs in one, the string of whose shoe I am not worthy to unloose), or is it a real Beauty—the interspersion, I mean, in stanza poems of rhymes from polysyllables—such as Eminence, Obedience, Reverence? To my ear they convey not only a relief from variety, but a *sweetness* as of repose—and the understanding they gratify by reconciling Verse with the whole wide extent of good Sense without being distinctly conscious of such a Notice, having rather than reflecting it (for one may think in the same way as one may see and hear). I seem to be made to know that I need have no fear that there's nothing excellent in itself which the Poet cannot express accurately & naturally—nay, no good word."

In this second epistle, "written," as Coleridge states, "five hours after the first," there is some account of Daniel, seeming to shew that in the meantime Coleridge had turned to the biographical account of the Poet prefixed to the book; but he does not retract his apparent inadvertence in speaking and thinking of his author as an eighteenth century man. This letter is a curious rhapsody, and we are apt to be rather mystified by the language of the writer, unless we are to infer that both communications were finished before the book was sent back to Lamb.

This is one of the periods of great obscurity in the career of the latter. We are aware that he was engaged in compiling and seeing through the press the *Adventures of Ulysses* and the *Dramatic Specimens*. But there is no letter between January 29th, 1807, and February 18th of the following year in the printed collections or in any other form known to me at present. With Coleridge himself there is no vestige of any correspondence between 1803 and 1809. Consequently the history of the loan of this book, and of the circumstances under which it again reached home, must remain doubtful, pending the possible recovery of new clues.

The letter from Coleridge to Lamb, respecting the tragical end of the mother of the latter in 1796, is printed by Gilman and Mrs. Gilchrist. It is of the most commonplace stamp, and might have been written by the parson of the parish.

This, with those in the Daniel, the one from Holcroft below, that from Jekyll printed among the Norris letters, and a sixth preserved in the *Memorials of Hood*, seem to constitute the grand total. It was a pitiless sacrifice. So late as August 31, 1801, all the letters from Coleridge at all events, which the recipient had kept, were safe; for in a letter of that date we find him forwarding them for the perusal of Manning. Can the latter have lost or failed to restore them?

Thomas Holcroft to Charles Lamb.[1]

[Dec. 4—5, 1806.]

"Dear Sir,—Miss L. has informed us you are writing to Manning. Will you be kind enough to inform him directly from me, that I and my family are most truly anxious for his safety; that if praying could bring down blessings on him, we should pray morning, noon and night; that his and our dear friends the Tuthills are once more happily safe in England, and that I earnestly entreat not only a single letter, but a correspondence with him, whenever the thing is practicable, with such an address as may make letters from me likely to find him. In short, dear sir, if you will be kind enough to speak of me to Manning, you cannot speak with greater friendship and respect than I feel.

"Yours, with true friendship and kindness."

[Signature lost.]

[1] Appended to a letter from Lamb to Manning, of Dec. 5, 1806, but omitted in all the editions. At the commencement of the same occurs, also left out: "Tuthill is at Crabtree's, who has married Tuthill's sister;" and there is lastly the address, "T. Manning, Esq., Canton."

UNCOLLECTED POEMS

UNCOLLECTED POEMS

It was my original design to have confined this little enterprise to a review of the present state of the Lamb Correspondence and an instalment in completion of the material for a new and more exhaustive edition hereafter. But the opportunity has presented itself from time to time of adding to my collectanea a few poetical pieces apparently not yet incorporated with the various texts, and it seemed worth while to append three or four productions of interest in this way before I parted with the subject—perhaps for ever.

The lines "What is an Album?" have been transcribed from a volume which formerly belonged to Mrs. Moxon, and which in its integrity had enshrined no fewer than thirty-two contributions; but nine only remained when it came under my notice.[1]

[1] See a full description of this book, so frequently referred to in the later letters, in Hazlitt, ii., 298.

To Samuel Rogers, Esq., on the New Edition of his "Pleasures of Memory."[1]

"When thy gay book has paid its proud devoirs,
Poetic friend, and fed with luxury
The eye of pampered aristocracy
In glittering drawing rooms and gilt boudoirs
O'erlaid with comments of pictorial art,
However rich or rare, yet nothing leaving
Of healthful action to the soul—conceiving
Of the true reader—yet a nobler part
Awaits thy work, already classic styled,
Cheap-clad, accessible, in homeliest show
The modest beauty through the land shall go
From year to year, and render life more mild;
Refinement to the poor man's hearth shall give,
And in the moral heart of England live."

"C. Lamb."

To Miss Burney,[2] on her Character of Blanch in "Country Neighbours," a Tale.

"Bright spirits have arisen to grace the Burney name,
And some in letters, some in tasteful arts,

[1] *Bookman*, May, 1893. There is, I understand, a verbal inaccuracy in the seventh line; but I have not been able to see the original.

[2] Afterward wife of Mr. John Thomas Payne, the eminent bookseller. She was the daughter of the Rev. Charles Burney, son of the historian of music. A copy of *Elia*, 1823, exists, with an inscription: "Mrs. J. Payne, with Elia's friendly remembrances."

In learning some have borne distinguished parts;
Or sought through science of sweet sounds their fame:

"And foremost she, renowned for many a tale
Of faithful love perplexed, and of that good
Old man who, as Camilla's guardian, stood
In obstinate virtue clad like coat of mail.
Nor dost thou, SARAH, with unequal pace
Her steps pursue. The pure romantic vein
No gentler creature ever knew to feign
Than thy fine Blanch, young with an elder grace
In all respects without rebuke or blame,
Answering the antique freshness of her name."
"C. L."

The following production was written in the album of Emma Isola.

"WHAT IS AN ALBUM?

"'Tis a Book kept by modern Young Ladies for show,
Of which their plain grandmothers nothing did know.
'Tis a medley of scraps, fine verse, & fine prose,
And some things not very like either, God knows.
The soft First Effusions of Beaux and of Belles,
Of future LORD BYRONS, and sweet L. E. L.'s;
Where wise folk and simple both equally shine,
And you write your nonsense, that I may write mine.

Stick in a fine landscape, to make a display,
A flower-piece, a foreground, all tinted so gay,
As NATURE herself (could she see them) would strike
With envy, to think that she ne'er did the like:
And since some LAVATERS, with head-pieces comical,
Have pronounc'd people's hands to be physiognomical,
Be sure that you stuff it with AUTOGRAPHS plenty,
All framed to a pattern, so stiff, and so dainty.
They no more resemble folks' every-day writing,
Than lines penn'd with pains do extemp'rel enditing;
Or the natural countenance (pardon the stricture)
The faces we make when we sit for our picture.

"Thus you have, dearest EMMA, an ALBUM complete—
Which may *you* live to finish, and *I* live to see it;
And since you began it for innocent ends,
May it swell, & grow bigger each day with new friends,
Who shall set down kind names, as a token and test,
As I my poor *autograph* sign with the rest."

"C. LAMB."

The following lines appear to have been composed for the album of another young lady friend, Sophy Holcroft, afterward Mrs. Jefferson:—

"TO THE BOOK.

" Little casket, storehouse rare
Of rich conceits to please the fair!
Happiest he of mortal men
I crown him Monarch of the Pen—
To whom Sophia deigns to give
The flattering Prerogative
To inscribe his name in chief
On thy first and maiden leaf.—
When thy Pages shall be full
With what brighter Wits can cull
Of the tender, or Romantic—
Creeping prose, or verse gigantic—
Which thy spaces so shall cram,
That the Bee-like epigram,
Which a twofold tribute brings,
Hath not room left wherewithal
To infix its tiny scrawl;
Haply some more youthful Swain
Striving to describe his pain,
And the Damsel's ear to seize
With more expressive lays than these,
When he finds his own excluded,
And their counterfeits intruded,
While, loitering in the Muses' bower,
He over-staid the Eleventh Hour
Till the Table's filled—shall fret,
Die, or sicken, with regret,
Or into a shadow pine,
While this triumphant verse of mine,
Like to some poorer stranger-guest
Bidden to a Good Man's feast
Shall sit—by merit less than fate—
In the upper seat in state."

"CH[s] LAMB."

The turn of Lamb for the acrostic set in at a late period of life, and he flattered himself that he attained considerable proficiency in the art of composing it. Some of those inserted in the printed editions are not quite accurately given; but I shall limit myself to copies of verses on the names of *Edward Hogg* and *Rotha.*

"An Acrostic against Acrostics.

"E nvy not the wretched Poet
D oomed to pen these teasing strains,
W it so cramped, ah, who can show it,
A re the trifles worth the pains.
R hyme compared with this were easy,
D ouble Rhymes may not displease ye.

"H omer, Horace sly & caustic,
O wed no fame to vile acrostic.
G 's, I am sure, the Readers choked with,
G ood men's names must not be joked with."

"To R. Q.

Acrostic.

"R otha, how in numbers light,
O ught I to express thee?
T ake my meaning in its flight—
H aste imports not always slight—
A nd believe, I bless thee."

"Charles Lamb."

These *nugæ* one is almost ashamed of perpetuating. Lamb thought that album verses were rather undignified; but he lived to find a lower depth, as he himself has put it in a letter to a friend.

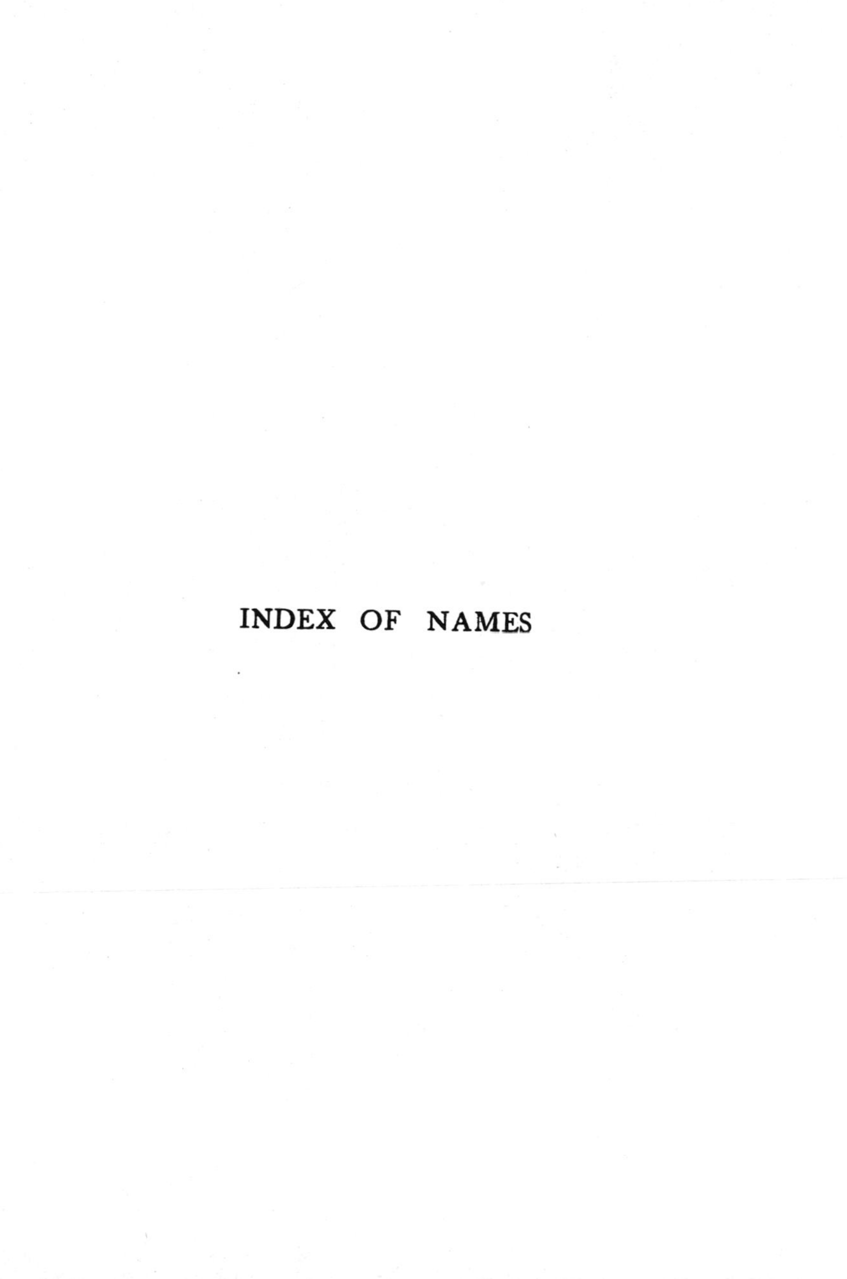

INDEX OF NAMES

INDEX OF NAMES

Abercrombys, The, 41
Ainger, Canon, 5, 20-1, 31, 83 *et seqq.*, 87-92, 95-6, 169
Ainsworth, W. H., 194-6
Alsop, Thomas, 14, 44, 177
Anderson, Dr., 116, 119
Bangham, Miss, 167
Baring, Sir Francis, 122
Barton, Bernard, 42, 44
Bartrum the Pawnbroker, 76
Bell and Crown, Holborn, 166
Bennett, Mrs., 213
Bethams, The, 94, 143-57
Bewdley, Worcestershire, 24-5
Bexley, 46
Bird, W., 5
Birmingham, 72
Black, Algernon, 40
Blake, William, 42-3
Brailsford, W., 48
Broadwood, James, 37
Brookes, Mrs., 196
Burneys, The, 34, 129, 230
Byron, Lord, 48, 54, 158, 231
Campbell, J. Dykes, 95
Catalani, 151
Chambers Family, 20, 36-40, 44, 53-4, 92, 95, 105, 137-41
Christ's Hospital, 8, 16-17, 22, 28
Cibber, Colley, 211
Clarke, Cowden, 44, 202
Coleridge, Hartley, 116
——— S. T., 12, 14, 18-19-20, 22, 28-9, 32-3, 35, 41, 43-4, 48, 61-2, 64, 77, 79, 95, 98, 111 *et seqq.*, 134-5, 150, 192, 198, 212, 219-24
Collier, Mrs., 142-3
Cottle, Joseph, 14, 32
Cottles, The, 32, 102-5, 120-1
Coulson, William, 76
Coventry, Thomas, 8, 25
Crabtree, 225
Crown Office Row, 29
Cuckoo, The (a Paris diligence), 171
Daniel, George, 78
——— Samuel, 219-24
Davenant, Sir W., 211
Dibdin, J. B., 20, 92
Dillons, The, 201-2
Dodwell, Henry, 20, 92
Dollin, Mary, 123
Donne, W. B., 190
Dowden, Isaac, 9, 105
Duncan, Miss, 151
Dyer, George, 18, 20, 22-3, 33, 43, 116-17, 119-20, 156
Edmonton (back of half-title)

Enfield, 21, 48, 180 *et seqq.*, 202-5
Epping, 187, 190
Eusden, 211
Evans, Mary, 35
——— Thomas, 35
——— William, 34-5, 54
Faints, The, 161-2
Fauntleroy, 77
Fell, 33
Fenwick, John, 33, 93
Field, Barron, 10, 166, 191
——— Frank, 166
——— Henrietta, 7, 29-30
Fields, The, 14
Fox, Caroline, 77
Galton, S., 79
Garrick Plays, 206
Gilchrist, Anne, 86, 224
Gilmans, The, 198, 224
Godwin, W., 32-33. 43-4, 77, 99-100, 118
——— M. J., 72-3
Grasshopper, Gracechurch Street, 205
Gutch, J. M., 32
Hancock the Artist, 15, 55
Hastings, 159
Hays, Mary, 33
Hazlitts, The, 8, 21, 22, 31, 33-4, 43, 48, 55-6, 64, 83 *et seqq.*, 94, 129, 143, 152, 192-3, 195-6, 216, 224-5
Highgate, 198
Hogg, Edward, 234
Holcroft, Thomas, 32-3, 129, 152, 224-5
——— Mrs., 146
Holcrofts, The, 169-76, 233
Hone, William, 44, 202, 204-7
Hoods, The, 166, 202-3, 208-10, 224
Hornidge, M., 53-4
Humes, The, 213-14
Humphreys, Miss, 95, 181
Hunt, Leigh, 20, 107, 136, 191
Hutchinson, Miss, 197-9
India House, 17, 51-5
Inner Temple, 75
Inner Temple Lane, 8, 13, 21, 29
Ireland, W. H., 10
Irving, Edward, 205
Islington, 121, 198
Isola, Agostino, 178
——— Carlo, 178
——— Emma, 178 *et seqq.*, 201, 203, 229, 231
James, Miss, 30, 165, 168, 171, 210-11
Jefferson, Dr., 169
Jekyll, Sir Joseph, 162-3
Johnson, Dr., 200
Jonson, Benjamin, 211
Jordan, Mrs., 152
Kelly, Fanny, 169, 171-2, 211
Kenneys, The, 20, 33, 44, 95, 165-6, 169-76
Knole, 160
Lake Country, 26
Lamb, Charles, 3 *et seqq.*
——— ——— Curate of Enfield, 48
——— Charles, Esq., 48-9
——— Elizabeth, 17, 41
——— John the elder, 5-7, 12-15, 28
——— John the younger, 8-11, 20, 93
——— Mary, 20, 30, 52, 56-7, 63, 118-19, 131-2, 145-7, 150-1, 155-6, 159-61, 188, 198, 203, 208-10
Landon, Miss, 231
Lane, Annette, 95

Lavater, 232
Le Greis, C. V., 12, 18, 20, 22-4, 43
——— Samuel, 12, 18, 22-3, 43
Library, Lamb's, 61 *et seqq.*
Little Queen Street, 13, 15, 18, 21-2
Lloyd, Charles, 12, 18, 19, 26-8, 31, 41, 72, 79, 119, 124, 127, 192
——— Charles the younger, 26-7
——— Sophia, 26
Lockhart, A. W., 22
Lyndhurst, Lord, 23-4
Macgeorge, B. B., 79
Macmillan the Publisher, 56, 216
Manning, T., 12, 19-20, 31-2-3, 41, 43-4-5-6, 50, 94-5-7-8, 127-33-4, 171, 175, 225
Marshall, 173
Marlowe, C., 194
Martin, Louisa, 106, 131
May, John, 121-2-3
Merger, Baron de, 171
Miller, Major, 38
Milton, John, 10, 200
Mingay, James, 75
Monkhouses, The, 197, 200
Montagu, Basil, 205-6
Morley, Professor, 75
Moseley, near Birmingham, 26
Moxon, Edward, 44, 166, 211, 212-13, 215-16
——— Mrs., 229, 231
Norris Family, 18, 28-31, 43, 148, 156 *et seqq.*
Novellos, The, 44
Ogilvie, Captain, 191-2
Ollier, Charles, 200-1
Oxford, 116
Patmore, P. G., 172
Paul, Kegan, 100
Payne, Howard, 33, 44, 170
——— John Thomas, 230
——— Mrs. J. T., 230
Pearson & Co., 79
Pemberton, Sophia, 26
Penshurst, 160
Penzance, 23
Phillips, Colonel, 34
Procters, The, 3, 15, 199
Pulham, J. Brook, 54
Pye, H. J., 210
——— General, 211
——— Major, 211
Q., Rotha, 234
Reynolds, Mrs., 148, 210
Rickmans, The, 35-6, 207
Robinson, H. C., 11, 30, 33, 42, 177
Rogers, Samuel, 211, 229
Russell Street, Covent Garden, 21
Ryle, C., 53-4, 215
Saint Valery-sur-Somme, 173, 176
Salt, Samuel, 8, 16, 75
Savory, William, 152
Scarlett, Sir James, 33
Scott, John, 192-3
Shadwell, Thomas, 211
Shakespear, W., 10, 53, 71, 78, 130
Sheepshanks, Archdeacon, 24
Sherlock, W. P., 216
Skepper, Miss, 148
South Sea House, 8-9, 19
Southey, Robert, 7, 12, 15, 19, 41, 43-4, 121-27, 136, 198, 207, 211
Starkey, Capt., 5
Stoddarts, The, 17, 20, 32-3, 44, 143-4, 178

Talfourd, Sir T. N., 3, 8, 14-15, 17-18, 84, 92, 192
Talma the Actor, 10
Taylor, John, 193
Thelwall, John, 33
Thurtell, 198
Todhunter, Mrs., 213
Tourneur, Cyril, 195-6
Trereife, 23-4
Tunbridge Wells, 159-60
Turner, Cecil, 177, 186
Tuthill, Sir George, 32, 46, 93, 225
Twopeny, Mr., 75
W . . n, Alice, 76
Wainewright, Griffiths, 41
Ware, 198
Watford, 198
Weathercock, Janus, 41
Weston, Thomas, 211
Whitehead, W., 211
Williams, Miss, 177
——— Mrs., 177
——— Mrs., of Fornham, 33, 42, 176-91
——— Rev. Mr., 176 *et seqq.*
Willoughby, Lord, 37
White, Edward, 40, 54, 191
——— James, 23-6, 43, 52, 191
——— ——— the younger, 12, 18, 22-6
——— Samuel, 24
Wilkie, William, 119
Wilson, Miss, 216
Wordsworths, The, 41, 43-4, 94, 118, 134, 136, 192, 212, 216
Yates, Susan, 74
Yeats, Timothy, 16, 74

NOTE.

THE RARER ELIANA.

P. 72-3. *Beauty and the Beast.* Since the remarks on p. 73 were printed, I have met with a copy of an earlier, perhaps the original, edition of this work. The title is as follows:—

BEAUTY
AND
THE BEAST:
A ROUGH OUTSIDE WITH A
GENTLE HEART.
A Poetical Version of an Ancient Tale.
ILLUSTRATED WITH
A SERIES OF ENGRAVINGS
AND BEAUTY'S SONG AT HER SPINNING WHEEL,
Set to Music by Mr. Whitaker.

LONDON:
PRINTED FOR MR. J. GODWIN,
AT THE JUVENILE LIBRARY, 41, SKINNER STREET;
And to be had of all Booksellers and Toymen throughout the United Kingdom.
1813.
Price 5s. 6d. coloured; or 3s. 6d. plain.
12mo. pp. 32., + title-page, eight beautiful plates, and 2 ll. with Beauty's Song set to music.

The date is only on the cover. There is no external clue to the writer.

At the same time there fell in my way a small volume, without any indication of authorship, but much in the style of the *Poetry for Children*, entitled: Simple Stories; in Verse. Being a Collection of Original Poems; Designed for the Use of Children. London, 1809, 12mo., pp. 44 + viii. and eight plates by C. Knight after W. Blake, in a different style from those in the preceding work.